Michèle Kahn

Crafts Around the World

translated by Christine Hauch

photographs by Jean-Claude Dewolf

ANGUS & ROBERTSON · PUBLISHERS

Angus & Robertson · Publishers
London · Sydney · Melbourne
Singapore · Manila

Copyright © Librairie Hachette 1975
Text of this edition copyright
© Angus & Robertson (UK) Ltd. 1978
ISBN 0 207 95678 2

Made and printed in Italy

Most people think that folk art is something to be found in museums. But if you look around the world, you will be surprised how many people still carry on traditional crafts as part of their everyday life. The Portuguese farmer carves wooden yokes for his oxen, the nomads of the Sahara weave baskets from grass, the South American Indian fashions a musical instrument from the plants growing around him, and children everywhere paint Easter eggs.

What about you?

Don't be put off because you're not a farmer or a South American Indian. You may not always have the same raw materials to work with, but almost everything in this book can be made from the odd bits and pieces lying around in drawers and cupboards. Those Easter eggs, for example. Don't just paint them: try decorating them with wool as they do in North Africa, with straw as in the Balkans or with split cane as in Poland.

Whatever you choose to make, don't be afraid to add a personal touch. Use the ideas gathered here as a source of inspiration for your own particular creations. You'll soon see how easy it is to model and make and mould and mend as they do in other corners of the world.

General hints

Going metric In this book you will find two systems of measurement. The first set of figures refer to the metric system and the second to the imperial. Wherever possible both sets of measurements have been worked out in round numbers, but remember that this means that the metric and imperial figures are *not* equivalent, so make sure you only work with one set of figures.

All the articles illustrated in this book are easy enough to make and there are detailed instructions for each one. However, it is not essential to copy them exactly. You can adapt them to suit whatever materials you have to hand and decorate them with your own designs. Some of the motifs illustrated may turn out to be too large or too small for the article you have made. In that case you can enlarge them as follows: trace the motif and cover it with a grid of squares measuring 5 mm/$\frac{1}{4}$" or 1 cm/$\frac{1}{2}$" depending on how big it is. Make another grid of larger squares and carefully transfer the design to the second grid, working square by square. To make the design smaller, work from large to smaller squares.

The author would like to thank all those who have helped with information, in the various embassies, at the Musée de l'Homme and the Musée des Arts et Traditions populaires, Paris.

Diagrams by René Mettler

Contents

Europe

GERMANY St Martin lanterns

The fourth century St Martin was supposed to have given half his cloak to a beggar on a freezing winter's day and so became a symbol of charity. Even now, in many towns in Germany, the children parade through the streets on November 11th to celebrate St Martin's day, carrying home-made lanterns and escorting a figure of St Martin on his horse.

Materials: black card or flexible cardboard and black paint, scissors, ruler, cutting knife or Stanley knife, glue, nail and hammer, cellophane in various colours (sweet wrappers will do), silver paper (from chocolate bars), two clothes pegs, 35 cm/14" flexible wire. To light the lantern: a small 4.5 volt battery; a wired socket; a 4.5 volt light bulb.

Rectangular lamp: cut the cardboard to the measurements in fig. 1. Then cut along the solid lines and bend along the dotted lines. If your piece of cardboard is not big enough, you can use the same diagram as follows: mark in the AB margin; fold at D so that E lies over B. Then fold at C so that D lies over B. The diagonal from F gives G. G is where to start the GH fold. Fold down and glue the top 2 cm/¾". Use the knife to cut out a design on each side of the lantern. There are some ideas overleaf but you could use many others, always bearing in mind the size of your cellophane. Smooth out the cellophane and glue it onto the back. To make the lantern shine more brightly you can line the inside with silver paper, cutting the motifs out of it so that they do not block out the light shining through the cellophane.

To make up the lantern, fold along the dotted lines, glue the base pieces one on top of the other, stick down the gusset AH and hold it with clothes pegs while drying. Make two small holes on opposite sides of the top, thread the ends of the wire through them and bend the ends back into hooks.

Circular lantern: cut out the cardboard as shown in fig. 2, fold down the top edge and decorate as for the other lantern. Shape into a circle, glue together along the gusset and hold with clothes pegs. Fold the flaps at the base towards the inside and glue them onto a piece of cardboard. Leave to dry, then trim the cardboard to fit.

To fit the light inside the lantern, cut out a second base to fit your shape of lantern, with a semicircular notch large enough to stick a finger in at the edge and a hole the size of the socket in the middle (see fig. 3). Line this base with silver paper. Make a hole in each of the battery contacts with a nail, put the socket through the hole in the base, thread 1 cm/⅜" of naked wire from the socket through the holes in the contacts and fold back. Then put the whole lot in the bottom of the lantern, screw on the bulb and it will light up. To turn it off just unscrew the bulb slightly.

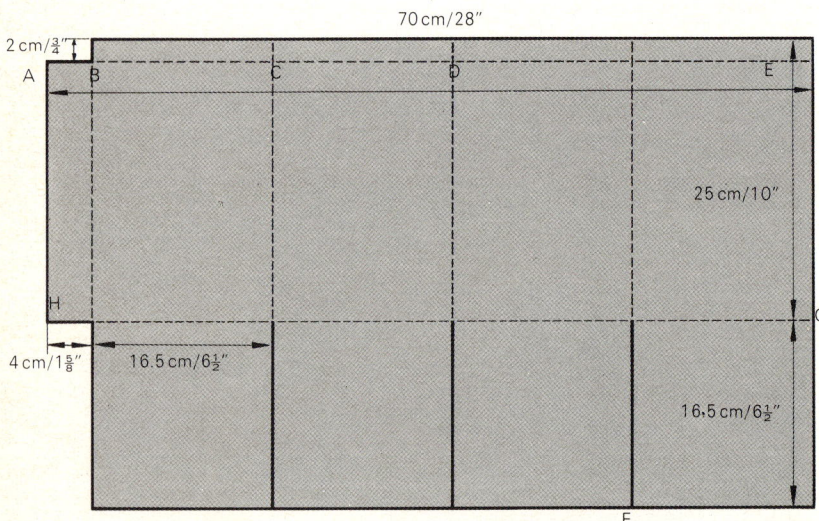

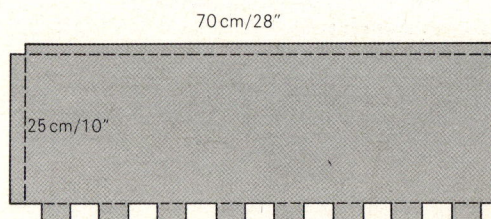

Light

BULGARIA Good luck charm

Following an old Bulgarian custom, friends and relatives give each other *martenectsas* (pronounced martenectas) on March 1st to mark the coming of spring. These little good luck charms are always red and white and usually take the form of twisted threads with pompons on the end. Sometimes the pompons are shaped into small figures as they are here.

Materials: two pieces of cardboard measuring 7 × 5 cm/3 × 2", medium thick red and white wool, scissors, sewing needles, very fine white and black wool, pieces of fabric for the clothes.

Hold the two pieces of cardboard together and wind a thick layer of white or red wool round them lengthwise. Tie up one end with a piece of wool and cut the other end with the scissors between the pieces of cardboard (see diagram). Tie round all thicknesses for the neck, trim a few threads on each side to form arms, then tie for the wrists and waist.

White man: wind red wool round the neck, across the chest in an X and round the waist and wrists. Stitch the eyes and mouth in black wool. Divide wool for the legs and wind black thread round the knees, down in a spiral to the ankle and back again, crossing over the first spiral. Cut a piece of black felt measuring 5 × 2.5 cm/2 × 1", stitch knots of black wool on it so it looks like fur and sew up the sides. Fix the hat on the head.

Red lady: stitch the face and hair in black wool and the neckline in white. Tie the waist and wrists in white wool. Put a triangular scarf on the head and tie the apron round the waist with a length of wool threaded through the top.

For the cord which joins the two figures, cut two pieces of wool 80 cm/32" long, one white and one red, knot them together and hook one end over something firm like a nail. Twist the free end as much as you can, unhook the other end and fold in the middle so that the twists

coil together. Sew one end to the top of each figure. If you want to wear the charm you can attach a safety pin to the cord and hide it with a bow.

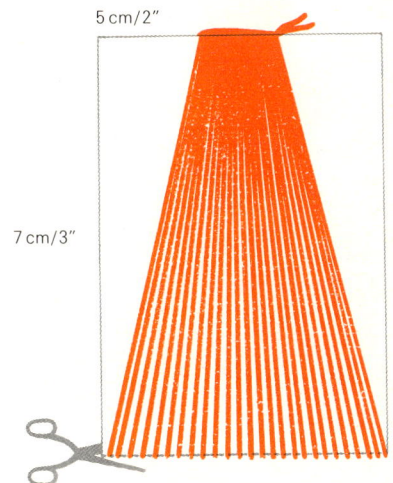

5 cm/2"

7 cm/3"

DENMARK Flying hearts

Christmas isn't Christmas in Denmark without paper hearts and *nisser* (small goblins which help Santa Claus deliver presents), which may be embroidered on their special table cloths, woven into baskets to hold sweets on the tree or hang loose as here.

Materials: bright red cardboard or drawing paper, 40 cm/16" florists' wire (or other flexible wire), red cotton thread, scissors, glue, tracing paper.

Using the designs below, trace and cut out sixteen large and sixteen small hearts. Make a small loop at each end of the wire and tie a length of red cotton to the centre for hanging up the mobile. Wind the loose end of thread round a piece of paper to stop it getting tangled. Tie another length of cotton to one loop and 2 cm/¾" below fix on the top of a large heart, applying the glue to the thread and pressing it in place with white paper. Glue on a small heart so that it hangs in the middle of the large one (see picture) and cut the thread. Stick a second thread to the bottom of the large heart and 2 cm/¾" below that add the next large heart. Continue until you have four large and four small hearts. Repeat on the other wire loop. Then tie a thread 7 cm/3" from the centre and hang up the whole mobile so you can see how flexible the wire is and work out the position of the first heart on this thread. Make the third and fourth strings of hearts in the same way as the first.

SPAIN Flowered mirror

Tin has been mined in Spain since the days of the Romans, when it was used to prevent other metals such as copper and iron from corroding, but the art of making ornaments from tin plate is not as well known outside Spain as it should be. Spanish craftsmen use the metal to make such decorative objects as this mirror and the brilliantly coloured cock on the frontispiece, which you can make yourself.

Materials: a mirror (here measuring 16 × 22 cm/6½ × 9") with no mount, thick cardboard, felt or adhesive fabric, 30 cm/12" nylon cord, piece of aluminium sheet metal or coloured metallic paper measuring 35 × 30 cm/14 × 12" for the frame, but allow a little more if you want to make some flowers from this also, yoghourt tops, one for each flower or group of leaves, orange stick cut to a point, sample piece of carpet to use as a surface when drawing on metallic paper, Evostik, craft paint for metal surfaces, brushes, ruler, compasses, small punch, paper fasteners, scissors, spirit varnish and white spirit.

Cut a piece of thick cardboard and a piece of fabric the same size as the mirror and stick them together. Make two holes about 6 cm/2½" apart centred roughly one third of the way down the card, thread the nylon cord through and knot on the cardboard side. Glue the cardboard to the back of the mirror.

Cut an oval of cardboard to fit round the mirror (see fig. 1), place it on the metal or metallic paper, add a 5 mm/¼" margin all round and cut out. Place the metal frame on the piece of carpet and draw a series of scallops 1 cm/⅜" deep round the inside edge, not forgetting to allow for the margin. Paint the metal frame, soaking the brush in spirit each time you change colour, add a thin coat of varnish and leave to dry for five hours. Glue the metal on the oval of cardboard. Notch the narrow border of extra metal round the outside and bend back over the card.

Shape the flowers from metal or yoghourt pots (some ideas are illustrated below), place them on the carpet and add the details with the orange stick. Paint the flowers in bright colours and add a coat of varnish. Work out where you wish to place them and punch a hole through the centre of each flower and through the frame underneath. Attach the flowers with paper fasteners. Stick a piece of fabric on the back of the oval frame and then glue the mirror in.

These flower patterns can be used for the cock at the beginning of this book.

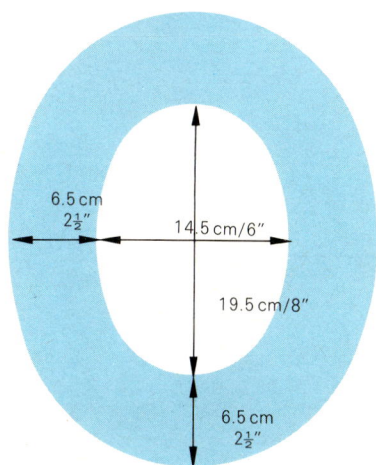

6.5 cm
2½"

14.5 cm/6"

19.5 cm/8"

6.5 cm
2½"

Measurements for a
16 × 22 cm/6½ × 9" mirror

17

FRANCE Weather-cock

In the days when horses were still used for transport and agriculture, almost every village in France had its own smith. He would cut and chase weather-vanes for the local houses and church from sheet iron or copper. There were all sorts of shapes. The most popular was the cock. This is traditionally supposed to be a reminder of St Peter's remorse on hearing the cock crow after he had denied Christ three times.

Materials: thin sheet metal 30 cm/ 12" wide in bronze, brass or aluminium finish: 80 cm/32" long for the body and the flag (bronze in the picture) and 50 cm/20" long for the feathers and compass points (brass in the picture), a curtain rod no more than 90 cm/36" long, a screw nut the same diameter as the rod, Evostik, thick cardboard, glass paper, stiff paper measuring 40 × 30 cm/16 × 12", all purpose scissors, cutting knife, pen-knife or small saw, coin, ball-point pen.

Draw a cock on the stiff paper or enlarge the one shown below (see page 8 for instructions). Cut round the outline, lay it on the metal and draw round with a ball-point pen. Cut out two metal cocks in this way. Then cut a third cock shape from thick cardboard with the knife, giving it a rounded head with no beak or comb and making the whole outline very slightly smaller than the metal ones. Rub the metal edges with glass paper.

Glue the card shape between the two metal ones, pinch in the beak and comb and carefully press the edges of the metal down over the card with the coin, except at the feet. Cut out the pieces for wings, tail feathers and eyes and stick them on. Trim the bottom of the card so that you can wedge it into the rod then pack the metal feet round the rod, holding them together with a little glue.

Cut two flags from the diagram in fig. 1 and glue them together. Bend the tongues over to form two pipes and slip the flag onto the rod so that it will turn freely with the slightest breeze to show you the direction of the wind. Then cut two sets of compass points as shown in fig. 2, slip onto the rod and screw on the nut to keep them in place.

You can put the weather cock in an upside-down flower pot or attach it to the window sill to show which way the wind is blowing.

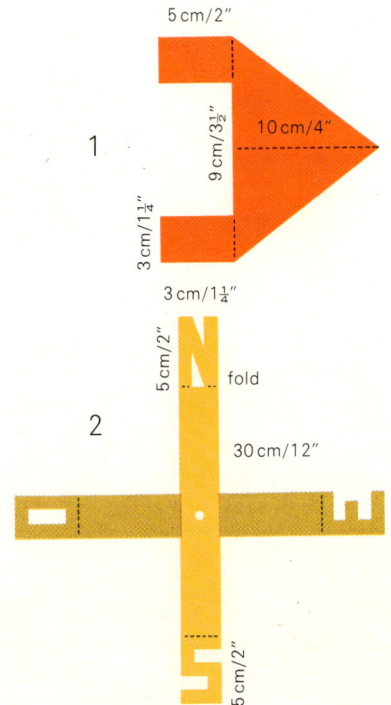

GREAT BRITAIN Pin cushion

In the days when Britain was one of the great sea-faring nations British sailors were renowned for their handicrafts. On long sea voyages they would carve objects from wood and whalebone, knot complicated macramé and make huge pin cushions like these to give to wives and girl friends as a sign of affection when they returned home.

Materials: an old, plain, preferably sky blue shirt in cotton or some other plain fabric, tracing paper measuring 30 × 25 cm/12 × 10", 100 g/4 oz cotton wool, scissors, pencil, needle and thread, small beads in various colours, fancy buttons, pins with coloured heads and nickel heads.

Fold the piece of tracing paper in two to measure 25 × 15 cm/ 10 × 6" and draw a rectangle of 22 × 14 cm/$8\frac{1}{4}$ × $5\frac{1}{4}$", with the long side AB exactly on the fold (fig. 1). Divide this into squares 2 × 2 cm/$\frac{3}{4}$ × $\frac{3}{4}$" and draw the half heart (see page 8). Cut out, unfold and pin on the fabric. Draw round the paper with a pencil, adding 5 mm/$\frac{1}{4}$" hem, and cut out.

Cut out another heart using the same pattern and turn under the hem on both. Tack. Place the two hearts wrong sides together and pin. Then, starting at the top, stitch together three-quarters of the way round, threading on a bead with each stitch (fig. 2). Stuff with cotton

wool until the heart is solid and evenly packed. Finish sewing up and take out the tacking stitches.

Decorate with beads, buttons, pins, braid or whatever you wish. Then write on your message with nickel-headed pins.

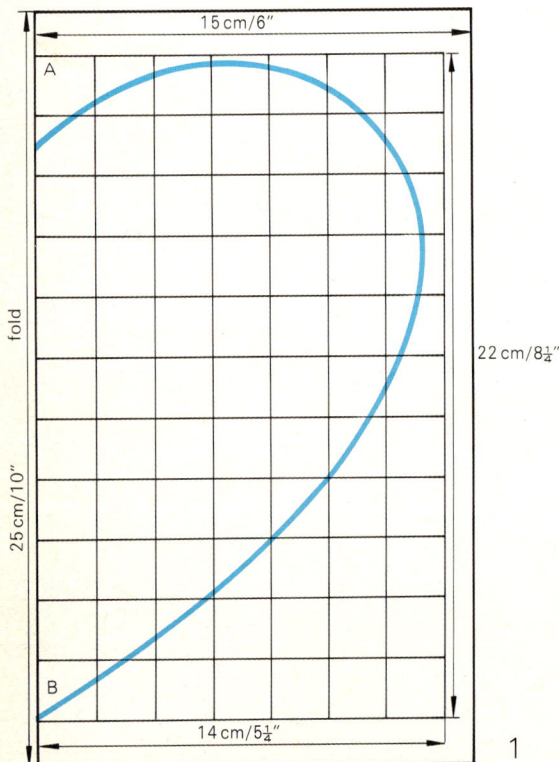

1

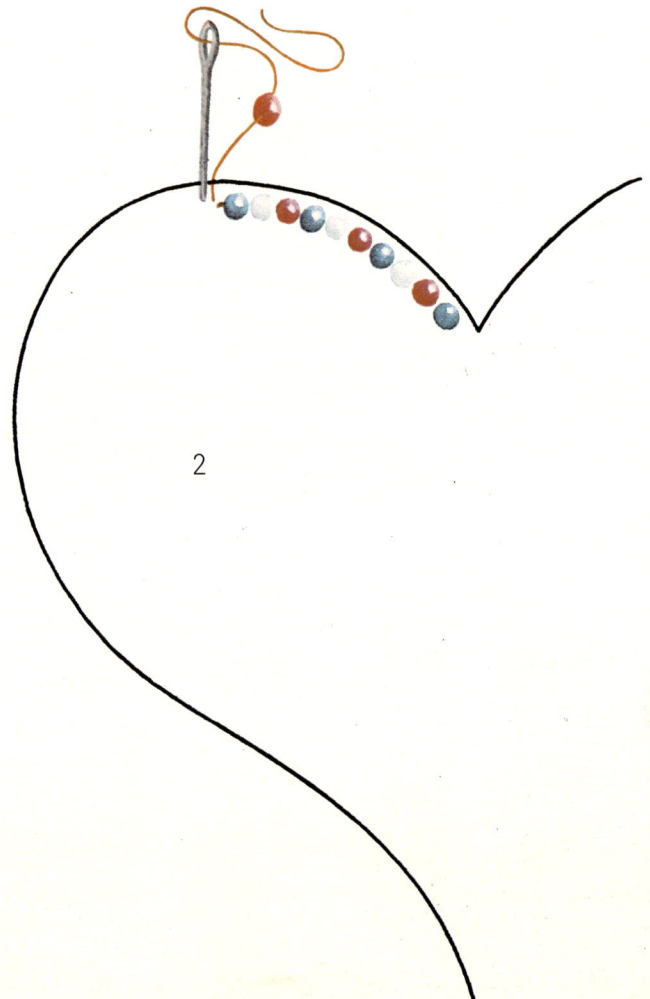

2

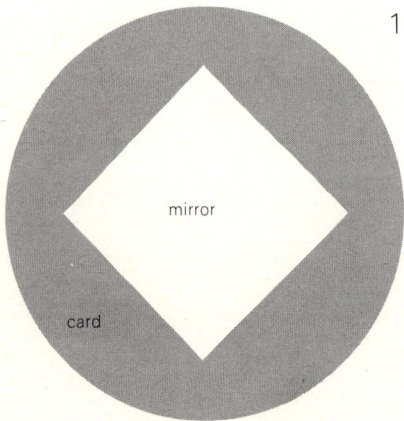

1

mirror

card

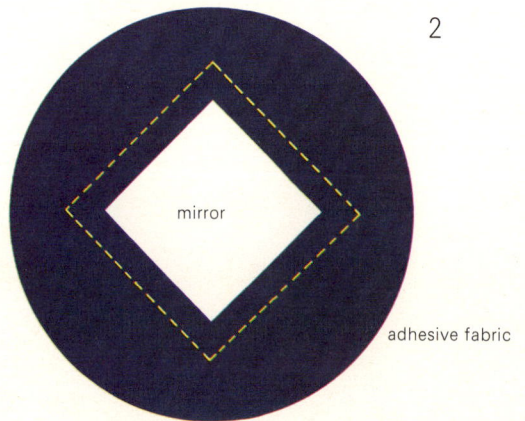

2

mirror

adhesive fabric

22

HUNGARY Mirror box

The shepherds of Transdanubia, a region of gentle hills, used to carry mirror boxes like these with them while watching the sheep. They would use them for shaving or for helping to adjust their magnificent twirled moustaches. Some of the boxes have a small compartment for holding moustache wax. The original from which this one was copied was carved and inlaid with coloured sealing wax.

Materials: a wooden cheese box (Camembert, for example), very fine glass paper, vinyl wood glue, a small mirror, cardboard, brush and indelible paint, clear spirit varnish and white spirit to clean brush, ad-hesive velvet measuring about 40 × 15 cm/16 × 6", depending on the size of the box, a small knife, pins, clothes pegs, scissors.

Clean out the box, but be careful not to get it too wet. Remove the staples with the point of a small knife, then smooth all surfaces and edges with glass paper. Glue the box back together again and hold with clothes pegs until dry.

Reduce or enlarge the design below as necessary (see page 8), trace and paint it onto the lid. Varnish all the outside of the box.

When dry, cut out a piece of cardboard to fit exactly inside the lid and cut a space out of the middle to fit the mirror. Glue both card and mirror onto the lid (fig. 1).

Cut four pieces of velvet, one for the base, one for the lid and two long strips slightly deeper than the sides of the box for the sides. Take care not to stretch the velvet too much or it will not stick properly. Stick on the side strips first and clip out notches where necessary to avoid wrinkling. Cut a hole slightly smaller than the mirror in the lid lining before sticking it on (fig. 2).

ITALY Dancing Harlequin

In the sixteenth and seventeenth centuries the Italian Commedia dell'arte attracted large audiences. It was a kind of popular comedy with stock characters such as Pierrot, Pantaloon and Harlequin. Harlequin was the young lover of Columbine and always wore a costume patterned in bold diamond shapes.

Materials: Bristol board or stiff cardboard, tracing paper, pencil, grey or black felt-tipped pen, paints, brush, scissors, linen thread, paper fasteners, punch or large needle, coloured paper (wrapping paper is ideal), lacy gold doily, photograph of a face.

Trace the various pieces on pages 26 and 27 onto the cardboard. Paint the right side yellow and the back black and cut out the pieces. Cut out and glue the pieces of coloured paper onto the pieces of cardboard and draw in the diamonds with a felt-tipped pen. As it is difficult to make a good face, use a photograph (of yourself for example) glued onto the cardboard head piece. Make a ruff by cutting the doily in half, folding it into a fan and clipping a hole in the centre. Glue on more gold for cuffs, buttons, shoes and belt.

Pierce small holes at the tops of the arms and thighs and large holes for the joints and on the hat (see diagram). Pass a fastener through the hole on the hat and tie a thread to the back to hang the puppet up. Attach the knees to the thighs and the limbs to the body with fasteners, leaving them loose enough to move.

Tie the arms together at the top with linen thread, repeat for the legs and then join both these threads together with a longer third thread (see diagram). If you pull on the third thread Harlequin will dance.

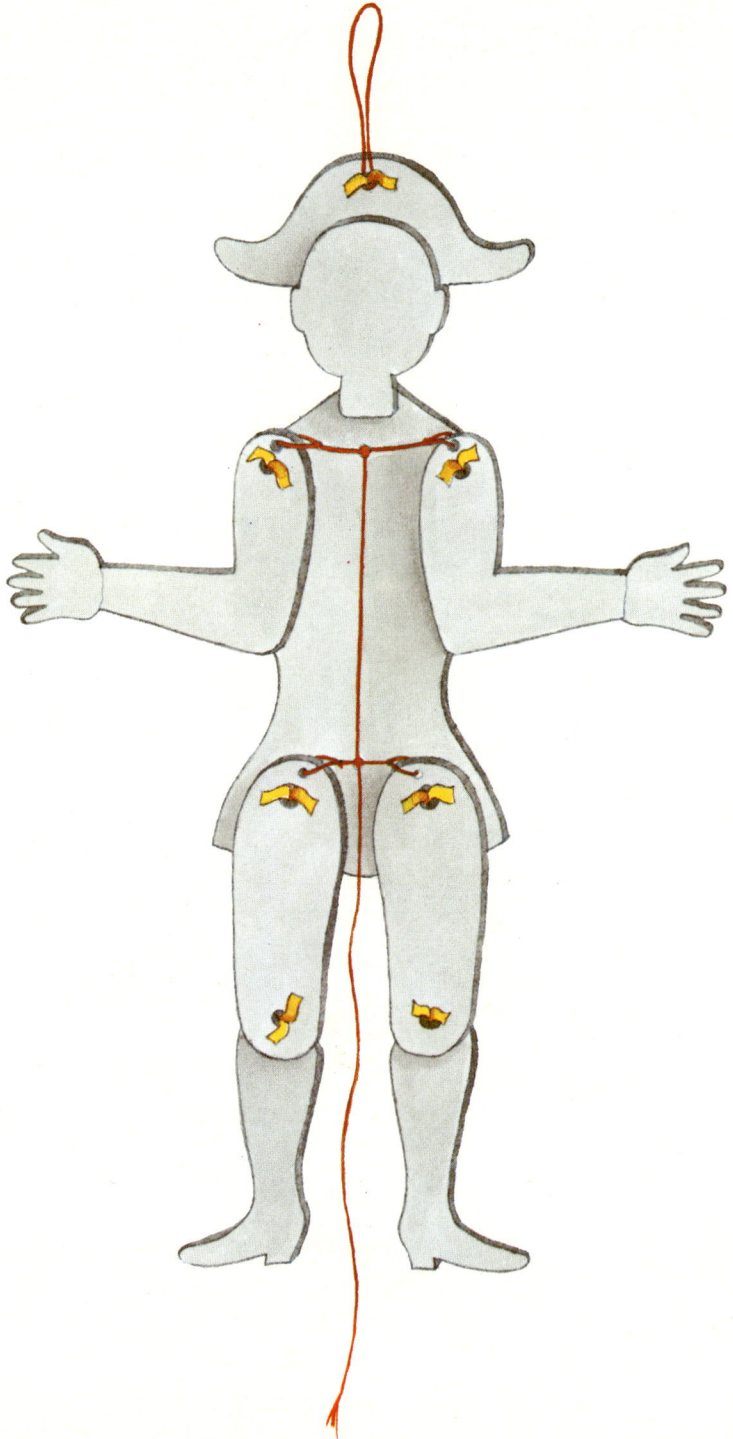

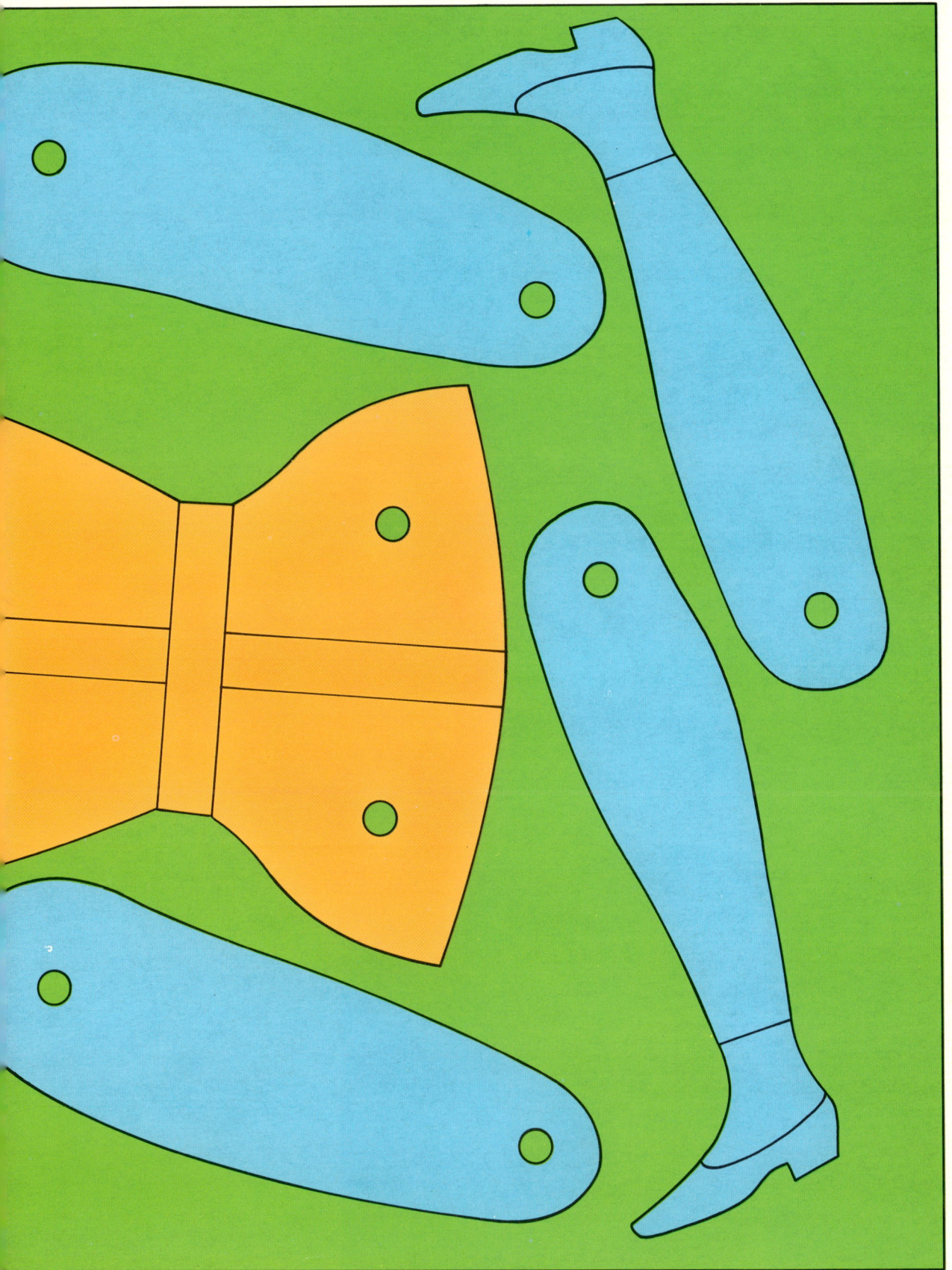

1

POLAND Paper cuts

Although folk art has been part of everyday life in Poland for centuries, paper cuts like these were not produced until the end of the last century when they were stuck on house walls for decoration. The delicacy of the cutting is amazing when you consider that some people make them with sheep shears rather than ordinary scissors, and that they probably used to work at them by candlelight during long winter evenings.

Christmas tree

Materials: a piece of hardboard or strong cardboard measuring 50 × 30 cm/20 × 12″, scissors, tracing paper, paper in different colours such as gummed paper, drawing paper, faces cut out of magazines on shiny paper etc, tweezers for handling small pieces, transparent glue.

Much of the work involved in paper cuts consists of sticking on top of one another pieces of paper which are roughly the same shape but of different sizes or with different detail. The branches of the fir tree on the following pages, for example, are made from triangles stuck on top of each other. For the symmetrical motifs, fold the paper in half right sides together before cutting what amounts to half the final shape. Cut by keeping the scissors still and manipulating the paper. When you have stuck on the pieces of paper press them down for a few minutes under a sheet of white paper.

Start by tracing the various shapes which go to make up the Christmas scene onto the piece of backing card. Then trace each small piece separately onto the back of the coloured paper.

For the woman, glue on the pieces in this order: face, hair, scarf, left hand, left sleeve, bodice, legs, skirt, apron, belt, right hand and right sleeve. The skirt and apron are made in one piece, then covered in vertical stripes and a black border. For the necklace, fold the paper in two before cutting as in fig. 3. The tablecloth is made from a rectangle measuring 10 × 3 cm/4 × 1¼″ folded in eight and cut as in fig. 2.

For the man, glue on the pieces in this order: face, hair, hat, trousers, boots, right sleeve, waistcoat, belt, left sleeve, left hand and turned-up cuff.

For the frieze at the bottom, fold a piece of paper in two lengthwise and cut semicircles along the fold. When your picture is finished you can hang it up as it is or frame it under glass with coloured passe-partout.

Book-marks

The designs on the opposite page could also be used for other things, such as greetings cards.

Materials: black card measuring 12 × 5 cm/5 × 2″ or white Bristol board and black paint, coloured paper, glue, tracing paper.

If you are painting white board, remember to paint both the front and the back black.

Trace the various pieces that go to make up the flower in fig. 1 onto paper folded in half and cut out. Glue on as in the diagram below. Repeat for the leaves. You can cover these book-marks with adhesive, transparent plastic to protect them.

2

3

fold fold

PORTUGAL Cross stitch

The Portuguese people love to have highly decorated objects around them. Their pottery is painted with figures and flowers, their regional costumes are bright with embroidery and their table linen is patterned with cross stitch designs like these. Young girls embroider hearts, flowers and birds on mats and napkins for their 'bottom drawer' to save until they are married.

Materials: red or white bolting or loose woven linen (35 × 30 cm/ 14 × 12" for one table mat, 40 × 22 cm/16 × 9" for one napkin cover, 30 × 25 cm/12 × 10" for one napkin), black, white and red embroidery silk, needles, scissors, ruler, pencil.

Table mat and napkin: embroider a border pattern 2 cm/¾" from the edge for the mat and 1.5 cm/⅝" from the edge for the napkin. The easiest way to sew cross stitches is by sewing a whole row of diagonals over two threads in one direction and returning in the opposite direction to form Xs. Draw the first few crosses of the design onto the fabric to help you position it properly. If you design your own motif, remember to work out the exact number and position of Xs needed. Fringe the edges by pulling off the horizontal threads and trimming the loose ends.

Napkin cover: hem one of the shorter sides, make a pocket 12 cm/ 5" deep and stitch up both sides. Oversew the raw edges and turn right side out. Embroider a border motif on the flap, then a centre motif. Finish the raw edges on the flap with a fringe.

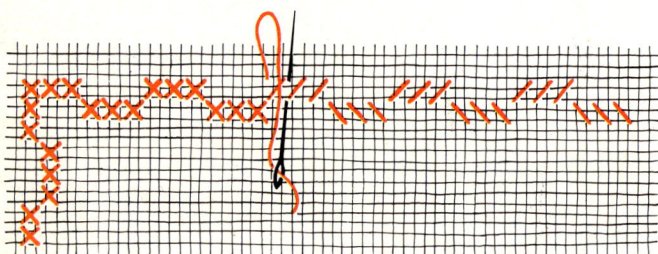

border pattern

RUMANIA Glass painting

Painting on glass was common in many European countries during the last century. It required less skill than putting together stained glass pictures and could be adapted for many decorative uses. Rumanian craftsmen were among the most brilliant in this field. Since the paint is applied on the back of the glass, there is no need to frame it in the usual way.

Materials: clear, uncoloured acetate film, gold paper, Rowney glass paint, brushes, cutting knife, tracing paper, glue, white card, ruler.

Cut out a gold background measuring 15 × 11 cm/6 × 4½″ and a piece of acetate the same size. Draw a framework the same size on the tracing paper and trace or design your picture inside it. Turn over the tracing paper so that the pencil drawing is back to front and place the acetate on top. Put a weight on one corner, outline the design in black or brown with a fine brush and paint in the colours, bearing in mind that all spaces left white will eventually appear gold. You can use the cutting knife to accentuate the main outlines or

make gold lines like the sunbeams on the top card in the photograph.

When the painting is dry, turn over the acetate and glue on the gold base. Glue the back of this to a folded piece of card to make a greetings card. You can also try this technique on, or rather under, a sheet of glass and add a coat of gold paint or place on gold paper to finish.

RUSSIA Nest of dolls

For centuries the Russians have carved marvellous wooden toys for their children: bears that dance when you pull a lever, merry-go-rounds that twirl as you wheel them along and nests of dolls like these. The traditional 'matriochkas' are made of wood but we can make slightly more fragile dolls from papier mâché.

Materials: cardboard egg boxes, bowl, Polycell paste, soup spoon, old nylon tights or stockings, thin string, sand, scissors, pointed knife, old flat plate, aluminium foil, file, very fine glass paper, newspaper, brush, pencil, paints, spirit varnish and white spirit to clean brush.

See page 48 on Indian bracelets for how to make papier mâché. Here we have used two egg boxes to make the largest and the smallest doll (16 and 9 cm/6 and 4" high) and one box for the medium size doll (13 cm/5" high).

Fill the toe of the stocking with sand and tie with a piece of string to form the head. Continue filling with sand until you have shaped the body, then knot the stocking tightly (fig. 1a). Turn the rest of the stocking

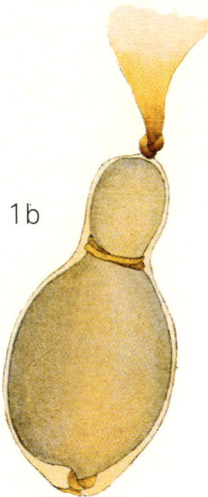

1b

back over the top and tie at the end (fig. 1b). Do this several times, finishing with a knot on the head. Cover this mould with papier mâché about 3 mm/⅛" thick, beginning at the head and reshaping the body from time to time so that it does not get bottom-heavy. Leave a hole at the centre bottom. For the smallest doll it is best to use a child's sock for the mould and then cover it with the stocking. When you have finished applying the papier mâché, place the doll on a plate covered with foil and leave to dry for at least forty-eight hours.

When it is completely dry, turn the doll over, make a hole in the stocking so that the sand runs out and pull out the rest of the mould. Draw a waistline about half way down the body and cut the doll in two with a pointed knife so that it will open like a box. To make the base, make a fresh batch of paste and cut ten pieces of newspaper larger than the bottom of the doll. Cover the base with glue, put on one piece of newspaper, glue again, add the second piece of newspaper and so on. Carefully cut off the excess and line the bottom with a piece of paper.

Cut about six strips of newspaper 3 cm/1⅜" wide to line the inside of the top of the doll. Starting at the neck, line the inside of the doll with them so that they overlap. The last strip should hang down about 2 cm/¾" below the bottom (fig. 2). Cover this in glue and fold it in three to make a flat pad. Cover the pad with another piece of paper. Make sure the top fits snugly into the bottom half and then leave to dry till the next day.

File away any bumps on the outside of the doll, then rub smooth with glass paper. Dust down well and draw on the main features lightly in pencil. Paint the inside black, then colour the face, hands and clothes. Remember to add the apron strings at the back (see fig. 3). Give the doll two coats of paint and one of varnish.

1a

string

2

3

SWEDEN Pine witches

Long ago in Sweden, witches played an important part in legends to do with Easter. Little girls would dress up and ride through the streets on broom sticks asking for sweets. Pine cone witches came out of the cupboard where they spent the rest of the year to take over the house.

Materials: a large pine cone, two egg boxes, Polycell paste, basin, soup spoon, vinyl glue, wool for the hair, pieces of fabric, one of them a square 15 × 15 cm/6 × 6", small bottle, coloured pipe cleaners, two small nails, six balls of plasticine (optional), paints, very fine glass paper, elastic band. The head and hands are made from papier mâché. Follow the instructions for this on p. 48 as for Indian bracelets, but using only one egg box.

Place the centre of the square of fabric on the top of the bottle and wind the elastic band round the neck to hold the fabric. Take a well-moulded ball of papier mâché the size you want for the head and push it down over the bottle neck. Then model the face: hollow out the eye sockets with the end of a pencil and put a pea-sized ball of papier mâché in for the eye, add a piece for the nose, carve out a long chin and draw on a grinning mouth.

Take a plain pipe cleaner, decorate it with three balls of plasticine on each side (see diagram) and shape a papier mâché hand on each end. Make sure the thumbs stand out well. When dry (this will take about three days) smooth down the face and hands with glass paper.

Cut off the top of the cone so that it will stand upright upside down. Take two of the cups off the other egg box, paint them black and nail to the narrower end of the cone.

Take the witch's head off the bottle and push the fabric lining up into the hole. Glue first the arms and then the head on the top, broader end of the pine cone. Paint the head and hands. Glue on a small skein of wool tied in the middle for the hair. Then dress the witch. You can make a broom with two pipe cleaners.

The small witches are much easier to make and less time-consuming. Just glue a ball of papier mâché or plasticine onto a small pine cone. Paint the face, add a few threads of wool for the hair and glue a scarf under the chin.

SWITZERLAND Elves

In the mountainous German-speaking region of Switzerland people once believed that the hills were inhabited by tiny elves who danced throughout the night. But because the elves feared the sunlight they vanished with the first cock crow and were never seen by man, though their footprints remained visible in the dewy grass and their invisible presence protected children through the day.

Materials:

Blue elf: pieces of fabric, light-coloured nylon tights or stockings, cotton thread, a little wool or felt, fifty small beads (2 mm/$\frac{1}{16}$″), two medium beads (5 mm/$\frac{3}{16}$″), compasses, linen thread, four sewing needles, scissors, vinyl glue, cotton wool.

Green elf: wooden bead 5 cm/2″ in diameter, four different coloured pieces of felt measuring 35 × 25 cm/14 × 10″, 120 small beads (2 mm/$\frac{1}{16}$″), four medium beads (5 mm/$\frac{3}{16}$″), compasses, linen thread, four sewing needles, vinyl glue.

Red elf: ping-pong ball, crêpe paper in two or three colours, fifty-five small beads (2 mm/$\frac{1}{16}$″), two medium beads (5 mm/$\frac{3}{16}$″), paint and fine brush, compasses, linen thread, four sewing needles, glue, awl or large needle.

All three elves are made by the same method which is shown in fig. 1. Four threads come down from the head, of which two are used for the arms and two form the body then separate to make the legs. The neck, body, arms and legs are all made by threading on a piece of fabric or paper and a bead alternately.

Green elf: glue the hair (fig. 2) to the wooden bead to form the head, so that the hole in the bead runs from the top of the head to the bottom. Cut four threads, two 40 cm/16″ long for the arms and two 70 cm/28″ long for the body and legs, thread them through the bead and make a knot at the top. Cut out twenty-three large (5 cm/2″) and 100 small (4 cm/1$\frac{5}{8}$″) rounds of felt. Thread three large rounds and

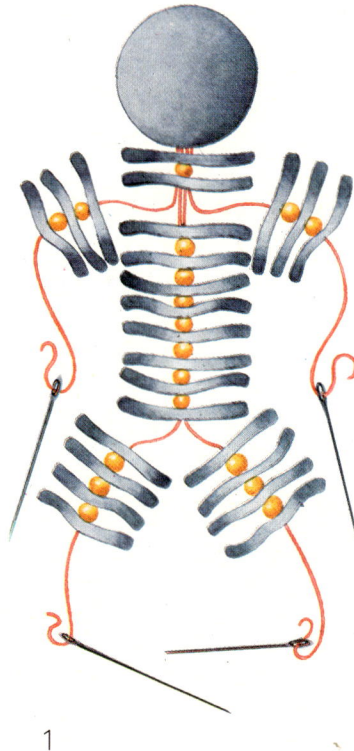

1

two beads alternately onto all four threads for the neck. Thread twenty-three small rounds and twenty-two beads alternately onto each of the shorter threads for the arms, finishing with a medium bead. Add twenty large rounds and nineteen beads on both remaining threads for the body, then twenty-seven small rounds, twenty-six beads and finally one medium bead on each thread for the legs. Make felt features to stick on the face and a felt hat from a triangle of felt stuck together to form a cone.

Red elf: this makes a good Christmas tree ornament. Make two holes in the ping-pong ball, one at the top of the head and the other at the bottom. Paint on the hair and face.

Fold the crêpe paper so that you can cut through ten thicknesses at once, and, treating these ten as one, cut ten rounds 4 cm/1$\frac{5}{8}$″ in diameter (two for the neck and eight for the body) and forty-two rounds 3 cm/

1$\frac{3}{8}$″ in diameter (eight for each arm and thirteen for each leg). Make up the elf as described above, finishing the arms with small beads and the legs with medium ones. Make the hat from a triangle of crêpe paper 14 cm/6″ along the bottom and 9 cm/4″ high and stick it on.

Blue elf: put the two toe pieces of the tights one inside the other and stuff with cotton wool to make a ball about 5 cm/2″ in diameter. Stitch down the ends. Sew on felt hair (see fig. 2) or thick wool (pieces of 10 cm/4″ fixed by the middle).

Cut ten rounds of fabric 10 cm/4″ in diameter for the neck and body and forty rounds 8 cm/3″ in diameter (eight for each arm and twelve for each leg). Gather round each round with cotton, pull the thread up tight to form a bag and fasten off. Then flatten the bag to form a circle.

Attach the four linen threads to the bottom of the head and make up the elf as described above, finishing the arms with a small ball of cotton wool covered in nylon and the legs with a medium bead. Embroider a face or make felt features to stick on. Make the hat from a triangle of fabric 18 cm/7″ across the bottom and 10.5 cm/4″ high. Sew it together, add a bell if you have one and stick it on with glue and a few anchoring stitches.

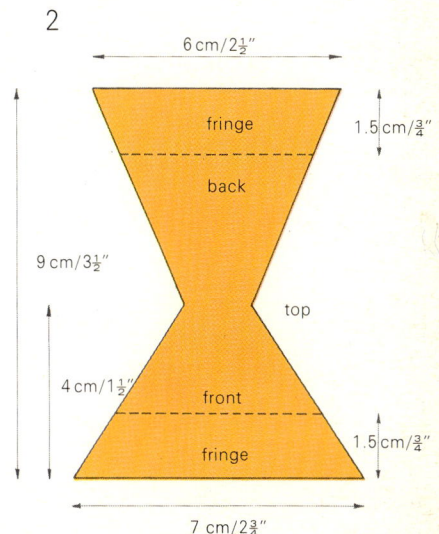

2

6 cm/2½″
fringe
1.5 cm/¾″
back
9 cm/3½″
top
4 cm/1½″
front
fringe
1.5 cm/¾″
7 cm/2¾″

CZECHOSLAVAKIA Easter eggs

The practice of decorating eggs to celebrate the arrival of spring dates back long before the Christian festival of Easter to the ancient civilizations of China, Persia and Egypt. The rabbit we associate with Easter is only a modified version of the hare which was the Egyptian god of fertility. Giving decorated eggs is still very popular in Czechoslovakia where delicate designs like these are common.

Materials: eggs, large needle to blow them, small cutting knife.

To paint the eggs: paint, brushes, egg box, spirit varnish and white spirit to clean brushes. *To dye the eggs:* food dyes such as cochineal, onion peel, saucepan and vinegar, dyes sold in chemist shops such as gentian violet, woollen rag, polythene or newspapers to protect the work surface. *For wax designs:* pure bees' wax (from the chemist), a pin in a cork, small tin can, saucepan.

If you want to keep your eggs for any length of time you will have to empty them by piercing each end with a large needle and blowing into one of the holes. Carefully wash the empty shells and leave them to dry.

The easiest way to colour the shells is with paint. Paint half the shell, place it in the egg box wet side up and leave to dry before painting the other half.

There are various ways of dyeing shells. For synthetic dyes like Dylon, dissolve the powder or liquid colour in a glassful of water and hold the shell in the dye bath with the help of a knitting needle. (Dip the shell in pure vinegar before dyeing for the best results.) Rinse the dyed shell well and leave it to dry. You can also use natural dyes like onion skins. Heat the skins of several onions in water with a teaspoon of vinegar. Immerse the shells in the boiling water. Depending on how long you leave them and on the original colour of the onion peel you can get yellow, orange, cinnamon or even red shells in this way.

Two techniques are traditionally used to decorate eggs in Czechoslovakia. The first is by scratching with a small knife. Draw the design on first and scratch it in with the knife held sideways so that the point does not break the shell. Varnish painted eggs, but polish dyed eggs with a woollen rag.

The second technique uses wax. The red and yellow egg decorated with geometric designs is typically Czech. Dye the shell with onion skins or in yellow dye. Put the tin can in a saucepan of hot water and melt the wax in it. When the wax is liquid, dip the pinhead in it and draw your design on the egg. Keep the wax at the same temperature while you are drawing. Then immerse the shell in a red dye bath, rinse and leave to dry. Remove the wax by lightly scraping it off in a little hot water. You will find that the parts covered by wax are the colour of the first coat of dye. If you want your design to be almost white, apply the wax directly to the undyed shell before immersing the shell in a dye bath.

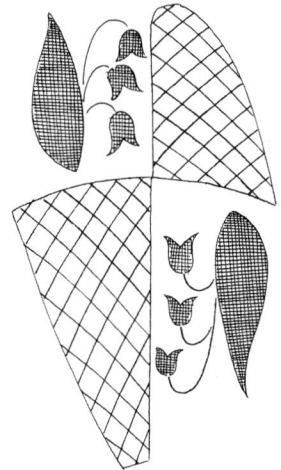

The photograph and diagrams show some traditional designs, but you can create hundreds of your own. To hang up the eggs thread a narrow ribbon through the holes and knot at one end.

YUGOSLAVIA Harvest wreath

Ever since man first started cultivating grain, farmers all over the world have celebrated their harvest. In England corn dollies are made out of straw. In Yugoslavia the women use grain and seeds to make hanging wreaths.

Materials: pliable cardboard, newspaper, old duster, pale linen thread, sewing needle, scissors, ruler or tape measure, pliers, sticky tape, seeds and dried vegetables (here 500 g/1 lb 4 oz red kidney beans, 250 g/10 oz maize, dried seeds of three melons and a pumpkin), to make a hole in the beans: fine drill (1.5 mm/$\frac{1}{16}$"), piece of wood or hardboard 10 × 6 cm/4 × 2", glue, thick cardboard, pin.

Make a base for the wreath by cutting a strip of pliable card 70 × 3 cm/28 × 1$\frac{3}{8}$" and forming a circle 60 cm/24" round with staples or sticky tape. Cut diagonal strips of newspaper 5 cm/2" wide, wind three layers of newspaper round the base as in fig. 1 and fasten with sticky tape. Cut bias strips of fabric from the duster, wind two layers round the wreath and stitch or stick in place with sticky tape.

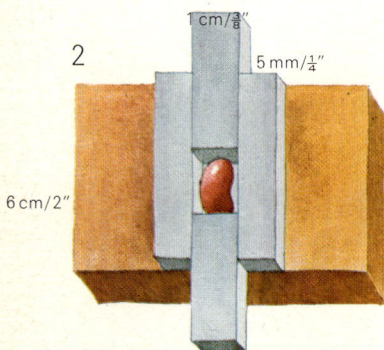

Construct a little clamp to hold kidney beans in place while you drill holes in them: glue three thicknesses of cardboard together to make four strips 6 cm/2" long, 1 cm/$\frac{3}{8}$" wide and 5 mm/$\frac{1}{4}$" high. Glue two of these strips onto the piece of wood 1 cm/$\frac{3}{8}$" from each other and slide the other two between them to fit the length of bean (see fig. 2).

Thread a needle with linen thread and thread on the seeds. Melon and pumpkin seeds hole easily, but maize can only be threaded in one way (see fig. 3): by pushing the needle into the whitish area and out the other side just under the tip. If necessary, pull the needle through with pliers. Wind chains of seeds diagonally round the wreath, stitching into the fabric from time to time. If several of you are working on the wreath, each one can make a chain to be stitched on.

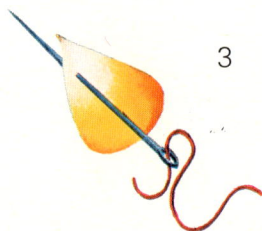

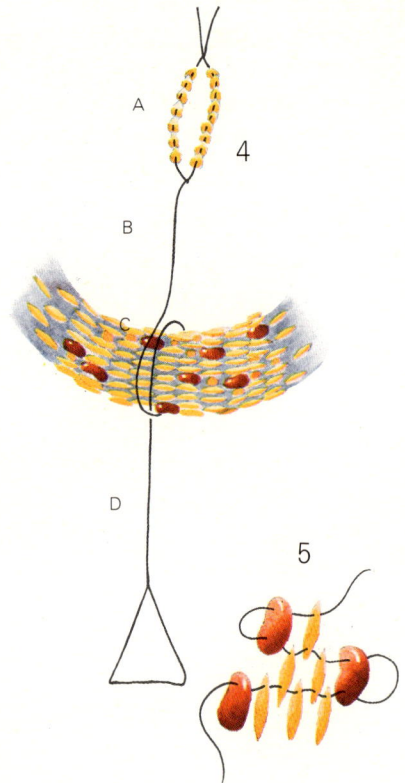

When the basic wreath is finished make a loop to hang it up by. Thread 20 cm/8" of double linen thread with maize and knot like a necklace. Take a 2 m/6' 6" length of thread and tie it firmly to the loop so that 1 m/3' 3" hangs down each side. Thread on about 13 cm/5" of seeds (AB on fig. 4), then wind the chain tightly round the wreath as you continue to thread on the seeds. Carry on for another 30 to 35 cm/12 to 14" (C to D) and attach the pendants of beans and pumpkin seeds (any long seed will do). See page 57 on the Philippines for how to make a triangle shape, which is just half the diamond illustrated on page 57. At the end of each row

add half a bean with two holes in it (see fig. 5) or two maize grains. Split the beans by pushing a pin into the small opening in the shell. Add extra maize or beans between each long seed on the last row.

Repeat for the other 1 m/3' 3" of thread, but wind it round the opposite side of the wreath. Work another 2 m/6' 6" of thread in the same way, winding it round the wreath to mark the other two quarters of the circle, and a final 1 m/3' 3" of thread to hang down the centre.

Asia

CHINA Tea tray

The Chinese use of lacquer, a varnish made from resin, to decorate wood carvings and furniture dates back over 2200 years. But, although trade with the Far East started after Marco Polo's first expedition in 1295, Chinese art was not really appreciated and collected in Europe until the 17th and 18th centuries. Chinese lacquered objects are found in a wide range of colours, some delicately inlaid with mother of pearl.

Materials: an old tray of metal, wood or Bakelite, or any cheap tray, emery paper for the metal tray or glass paper for the wood tray, flat brush 3 to 4 cm/1 to 1½" wide, water-colour brushes, tracing paper, ruler, sheet of white carbon paper or stick of white chalk, white spirit, black, red, gold and white enamel lacquer paint.

Polish the surface to be painted very carefully with emery paper if it is metal, glass paper if wood. (You can paint directly on Bakelite.)

Lacquer the back of the tray with the flat brush. Leave to dry away from dust for about twelve hours, then paint the top. Leave overnight until completely dry. To add the design, start by pricking out the outline of the diagram below (or any other design) on the tracing paper. Centre it on the tray, slip a piece of white carbon paper underneath (or cover the back of the tracing paper with white chalk) and transfer the design by going over it again.

Paint in the large areas of colour. Then, leaning your hand on a ruler or a stick placed across the tray, fill in the details with a fine brush. Leave to dry for twenty-four hours. Clean your brushes with white spirit and close the pots of lacquer tightly so that you can use what is left for the Japanese lacquer work on page 54.

INDIA Feather-light bracelets

The Indians weave a fantastic variety of beautiful fabrics to make their graceful saris. And to go with them they make an equally wide range of jewellery, from gold and silver, enamel, inlaid with tiny mirrors which glint like precious stones, and papier mâché. Darker colours like these are associated with the Punjab region in the north.

Materials: porous cardboard egg boxes, Polycell paste, thin card (e.g. manilla envelope), two basins, soup spoon, metal file or very fine glass paper, small cylindrical bottle or glass, paint, spirit varnish, brushes and white spirit to clean, white carbon paper or white chalk, tracing paper, cooking oil.

Papier mâché: prepare the mixture forty-eight hours before you want to use it. Take the label off the egg box. Break the box into very small pieces, ideally almost to a powder, in one of the basins. Cover with hot water and leave to soak until you can make a small, well-squeezed ball of the mixture which keeps its shape.

Drain the mixture gradually. Put five soup spoons of water into the second basin and sprinkle in a level soup spoon of paste powder. Stir till the glue is like thick cream and break the drained paper into the glue. Stir until well blended.

Bracelets: one egg box will make two or three bracelets. Holding your thumb in your palm measure round your knuckles. Add another 1.5 cm/$\frac{5}{8}$" and make a card bracelet that length and 2.5 cm/1" wide.

Cover the inside of the card bracelet with a thin layer of papier mâché. Apply it in small blobs and smooth them together with your finger. Place the bracelet over the bottle and cover the outside with papier mâché. Use the spoon handle to get a smooth surface.

Leave to dry for about an hour, carefully remove the bracelet, cover the bottle with oil and replace the bracelet. Leave to dry for between thirty-six and forty-eight hours, depending on the thickness of the bracelet. Use any remaining papier mâché straight away, to make another bracelet, perhaps, a small heart-shaped pendant or anything else which takes your fancy.

When the bracelet is quite dry file away any bumps and round the edges. Paint inside and out in the same colour. Light colours look best on an undercoat of white. The designs below were inspired by Indian art but you can choose any pattern you like.

Draw the design on a strip of tracing paper the size of the bracelet, then transfer it to the bracelet with white carbon paper or by coating the back of the tracing paper with white chalk. You could also paint flowers on and outline them with gold. Apply two coats of paint and two of varnish.

INDONESIA

Shadow puppet

Originally made of leather or metal, with movable arms, the *wayangs* (shadow puppets) of Indonesia were used to bring the great epic stories of Asia and the East Indies alive. Although limited in movement, the puppets were given specific facial expressions and clothes so that the audience would be able to tell at a glance whom they represented and whether they were meant to be heroes or villains.

Materials: stiff but easily cut card, scissors, tracing paper, pencil, paint and two brushes, one medium, one fine, a piece of thin bamboo or any stick 30 cm/12″ long, sticky tape, pin.

Trace the diagram of the demon with all his features onto the card, enlarging it if you wish (see page 8). Cut out and paint carefully. Then paint the back black.

Prick out the main features of the character with the pin. Attach the bamboo to the back of the left leg with sticky tape.

To make the puppet perform, place it behind a screen of white fabric and in front of a light.

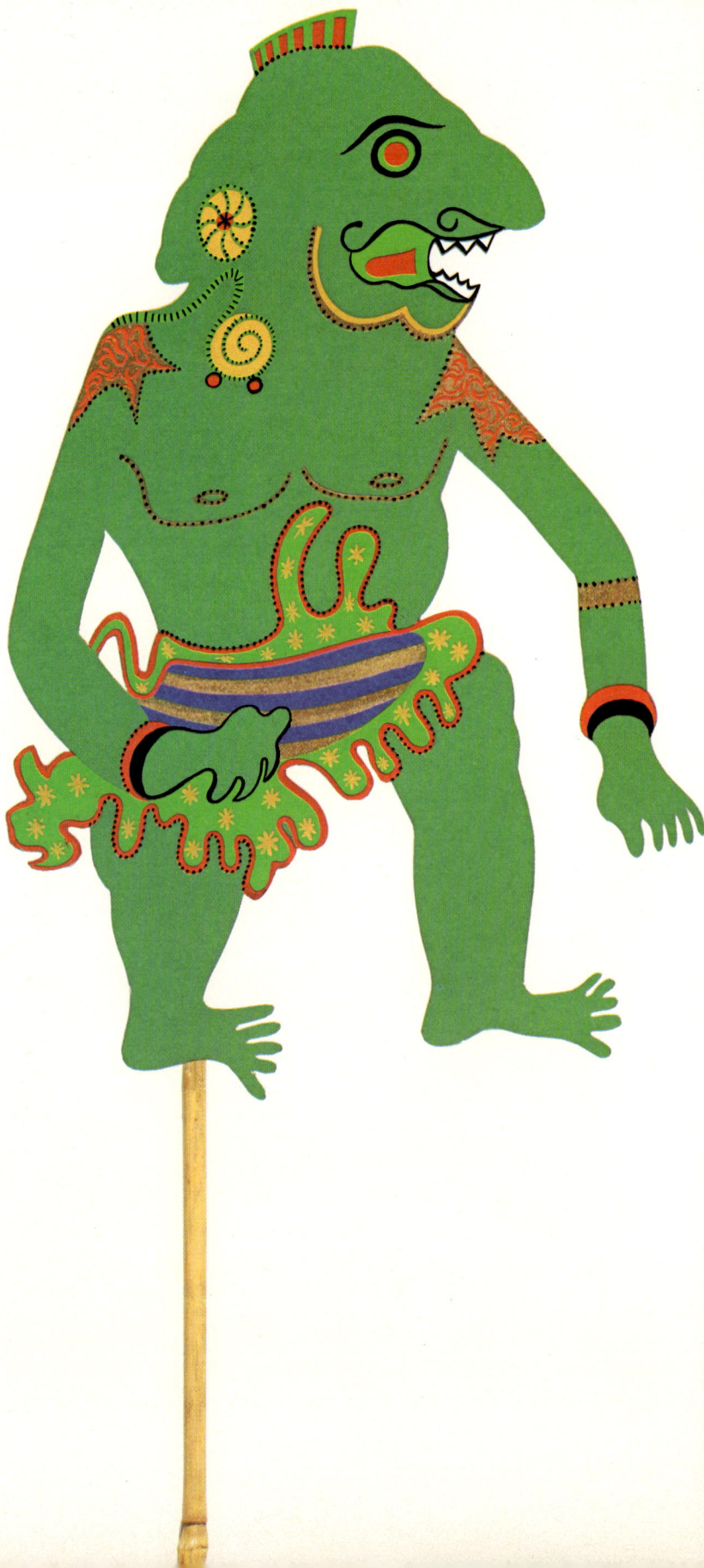

IRAN Miniature chest

Most of us tend to think of Islamic art as geometric in design, like the patterns found on rich, silk carpets and in mosques. But Muslim manuscripts were once full of beautiful paintings in jewel-like colours, called miniatures not originally because of their size but because they were painted in *minium* or vermilion paint.

Materials: a wooden or cardboard box, newspaper, Polycell paste, bowl, soup spoon, aluminium foil, very fine glass paper, craft paint, brushes, reproduction of a Persian miniature or flower patterns cut from a magazine, very fine, pointed scissors, transparent glue, spirit varnish and white spirit for cleaning brushes.

The best base for this is a cigar box with a hinged lid which just sits on top of the lower part without fitting into it. Cut six pieces of newspaper to fit each of the outside surfaces, three pieces for each of the inside surfaces and two strips 2 cm/¾" wide for each of the rims.

Make up the Polycell paste in the basin with a level soup spoon of paste to five spoons of water and cover the box with glued paper. Start with the flat surfaces, alternate with the rim strips and finish with the flat surfaces. If you want the top of the lid to look padded you can add a couple more sheets there. Cut a piece of foil larger than the lid, slide it under the lid and leave the box to dry for about forty-eight hours with the lid down under some heavy object. When the paper is completely dry smooth away any bumps with glass paper. Paint the lid with two coats of light-coloured paint. Draw a frame using all or part of the design below and paint all surfaces surrounding the picture, including the inside, with dark paint. Make up a picture with the reproduction and glue it carefully onto the lid. Varnish the whole box.

ISRAEL Candlestick

This is a smaller version of the nine-branched candlestick which is part of the emblem of the state of Israel. According to the Judaic scriptures, Judas Maccabeus was sent to reconsecrate the desecrated temple of the Jews by lighting a candle there. He could only find a small piece of tallow, but, miraculously, it remained alight for eight days. So the ceremonial candlestick of the Jews was given nine branches, one for each day the candle burnt and one for the original light.

Materials: a piece of 5 mm/$\frac{3}{16}$" thick hardboard or plywood measuring 45 × 37 cm/18 × 15", various dried vegetables (100 g/ 4 oz green split peas, 250 g/10 oz yellow lentils, about 50 popcorn grains and 50 red kidney beans, 100 g/4 oz green lentils), small mustard pot lid, tweezers for handling the grains, glue, spirit varnish, brush and white spirit to clean it, ruler, pencil.

Start by drawing a marker line down the centre of the board. Tip some glue into the mustard pot lid, dab a little on the dried vegetables with the brush and stick them on the board to form the lowest rosette of the candlestick about 7 cm/2$\frac{3}{4}$" from the bottom. Work up the candlestick following fig. 2, adding the base, the branches and finally the candles (here two halves of kidney bean). To split kidney beans, push a pin into the hole in their shell. Form a dark frame with half kidney beans. Fill the background by pouring a little glue onto the backing, tipping the lentils on and smoothing them down flat. Varnish the whole picture, leave to dry and stick a hook on the back to hang it on the wall.

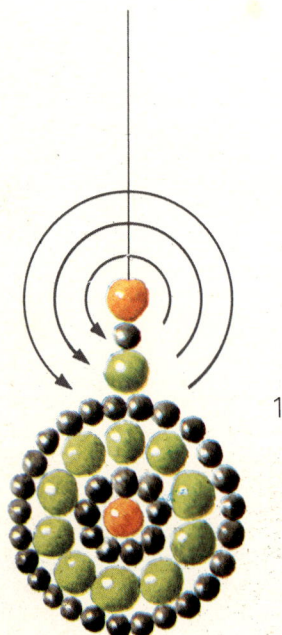

1

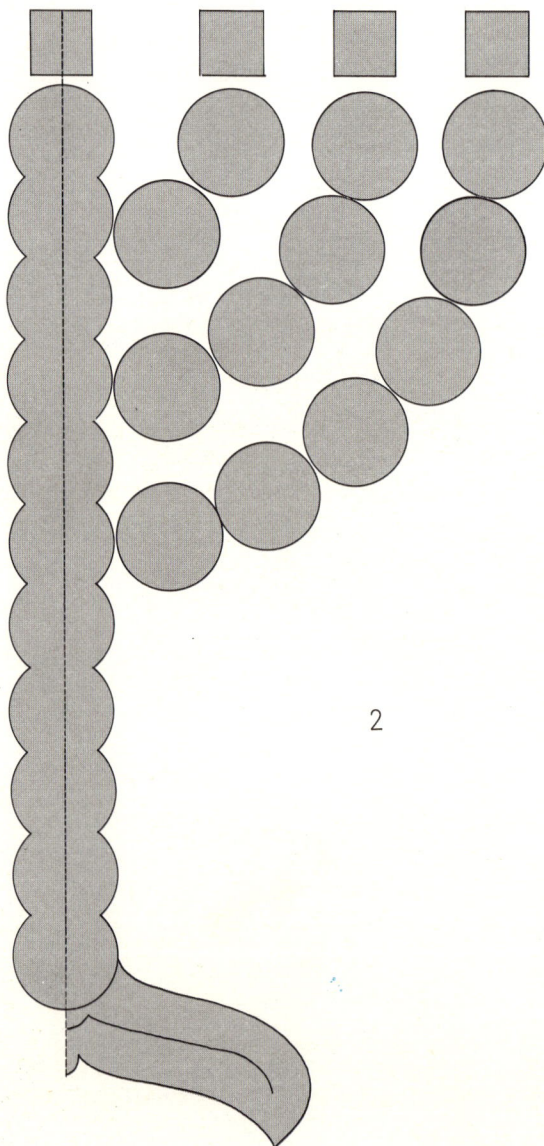

2

52

JAPAN Lacquered work

The technique of lacquering probably travelled from China, by way of Korea, to Japan about 2000 years ago. Unlike the Chinese craftsmen, the Japanese regarded lacquer as an art form and boasted a series of Masters of Lacquer who even applied it to temples and other buildings.

Materials: boxes, bottles or anything you wish to paint, enamel lacquer paint, flat brush and fine brush, white spirit, glass paper, white carbon paper or white chalk, tracing paper.

Rub the objects with glass paper until clean and smooth. You may not be able to paint the whole object at one go, especially if you want to cover the inside, so leave each coat in a dust-free place to dry for at least four hours, preferably overnight. When the background (traditionally black, red or gold) is finished, draw on your design with white carbon paper or tracing paper covered with white chalk. Paint in the design, ideally in gold if the background is red or black.

Be sure to close the bottles of lacquer tightly after use, then you can use them for other things.

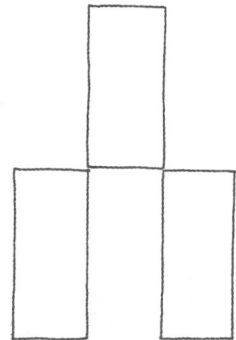

PHILIPPINES Summer necklaces

For special occasions Philippino women wear bright dresses with wing-like sleeves which make them look like tropical butterflies. They also fashion necklaces out of the shiny, coffee-coloured fruits of local trees. In our more temperate climate we can use melon seeds in the same way.

Materials: the seeds of a medium-sized melon, a needle, beige linen thread. For dyeing: cold dye, fixative and a basin or paint, varnish and white spirit to clean the brushes.

Wash and dry the seeds before use. Then make your necklace in any combination you wish of the following three methods: the chain, the diamond, the flower.

For the chain, follow fig. 1. Start by threading on A and B seeds through the top, B through the bottom, C and D through the top, A through the bottom, D through the bottom, E and F through the top and so on, backwards and forwards.

For the diamond, follow fig. 2. Thread on two seeds for the first row, three for the second and so on till you reach the fifth row (six seeds). Then thread on five in the sixth row, four in the seventh and so on to the ninth row. Continue working in a chain.

For the flower, follow fig. 3. Thread on the tops of A and B, the bottom of B, the tops of C and D and A, D

and C again through the bottom. Add eight seeds (E to L) and work round from D to G again. Go through the bottom of H and work five rows of chain before starting the next flower.

You could dye your necklace in the same bath as for a coil belt (see page 86). Leave the necklace soaking for an hour and a half, rinse well and dry flat on absorbent paper. You could also colour the necklace with paint and add a layer of varnish.

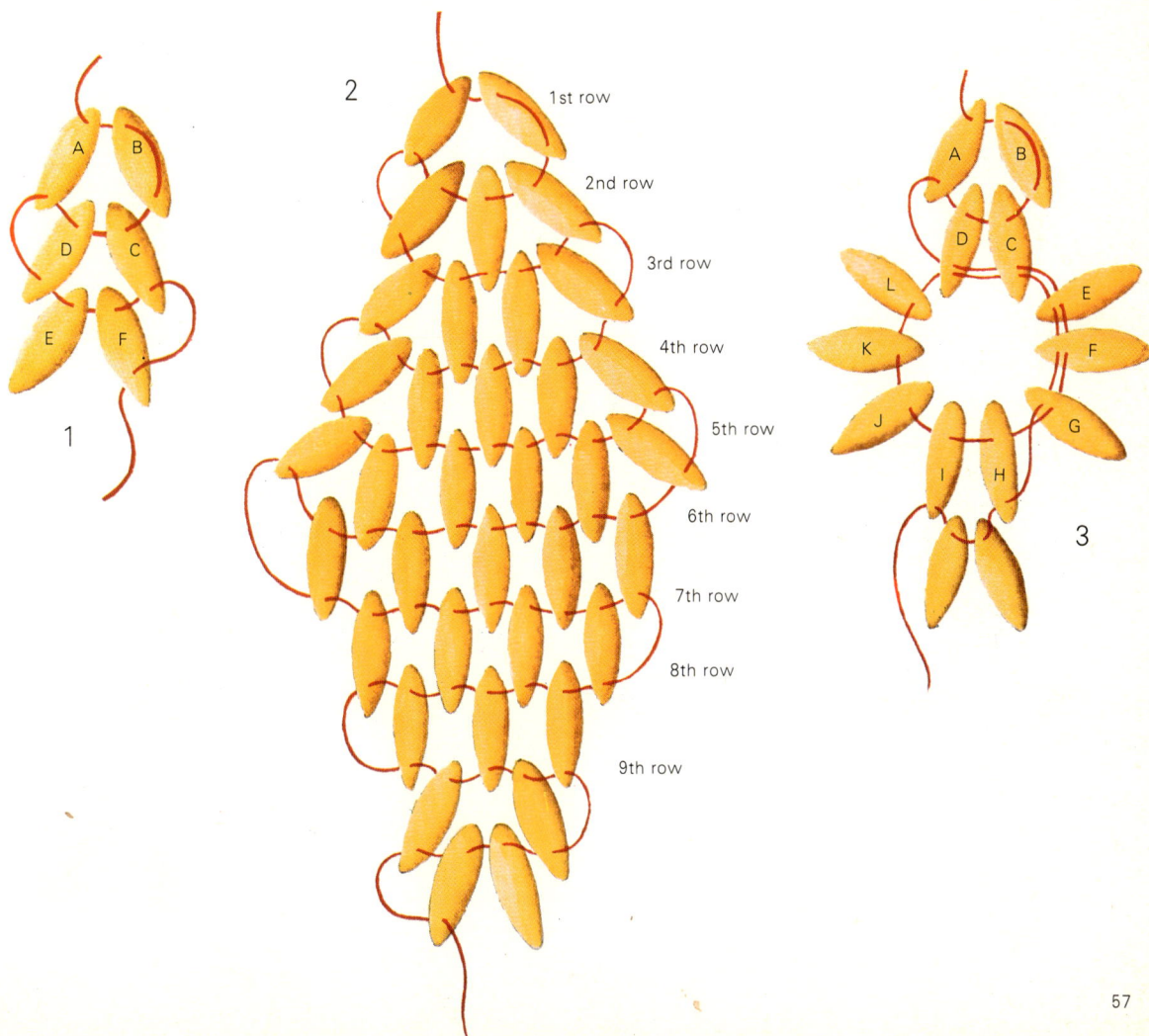

THAILAND Rosebuds

In a country where some of the most beautiful silk fabrics are woven, the people celebrate their religious festivals with fireworks, paper dragons and delicate flowers made of silk.

Materials: wire, pieces of thin, silky fabric, threads to match, green crêpe paper, stick of glue, pliers, scissors, ruler, compasses.

Cut a stem of wire about 50 cm/20" long and pull it out straight with a rag. Cut a round of fabric to 10 cm/4" in diameter and a piece of matching thread about 20 cm/8" long.

Fold the fabric in two as in fig. 1, and slide the wire into the middle. Continue folding as in figs 2, 3 and 4. Make a slip knot in the thread and pull it tight round the fabric 5 mm/¼" from the bottom. Bind down over the end and knot the thread round the stem.

Cut a strip of crêpe paper on the bias about 70 cm/28" long and 1.5 cm/⅝" wide. Place the paper on the stalk so that the lines in the paper run parallel to the stem (fig. 5) and wind tightly round the bottom of the bud. Finish with a blob of glue when you have wound the paper right down the stem. If the paper is too short join in another piece.

Long branch: working as for the rosebud, make five buds from green fabric 6 cm/2½" in diameter; attach one to the top of a wire stem about 75 cm/30" long and wind the crêpe paper down till you reach the position of the next bud. Tie this on with thread and continue winding round the paper. Repeat to the end of the stem.

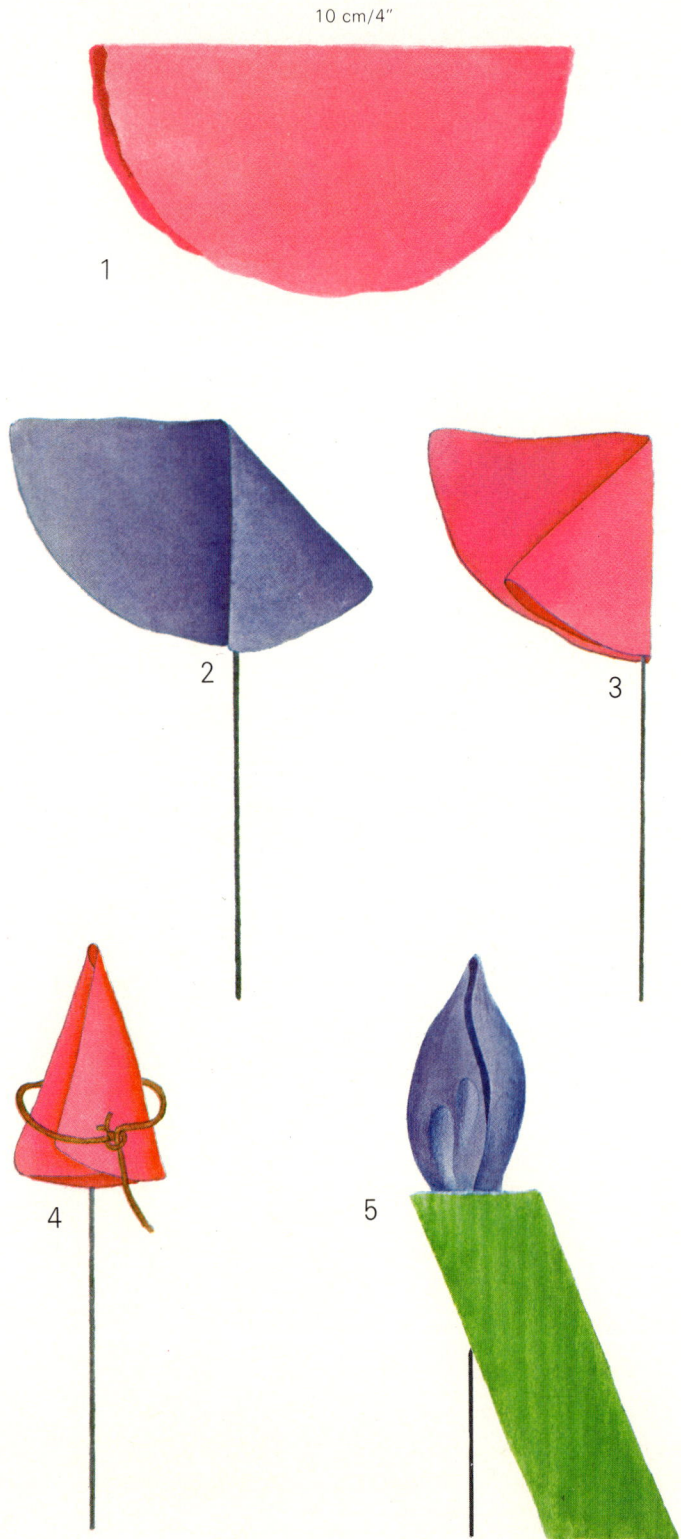

10 cm/4"

1

2

3

4

5

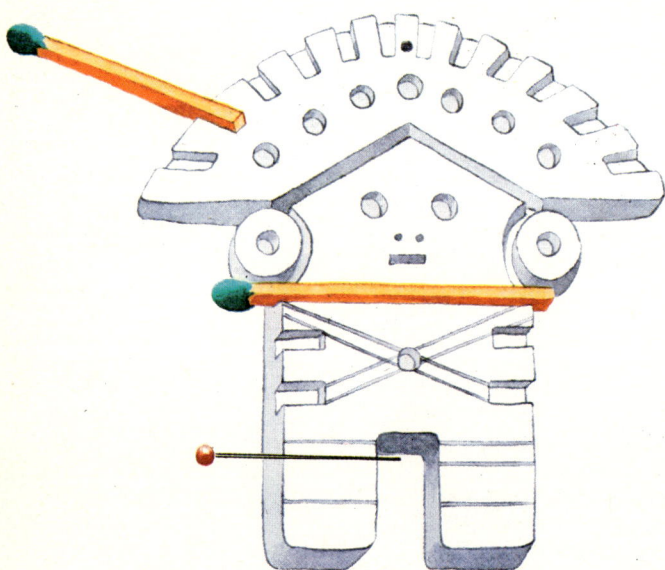

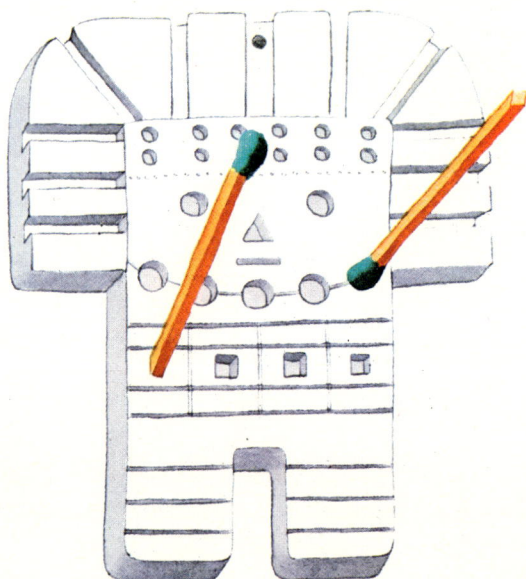

The Americas

BOLIVIA Inca warriors

The Quechua Indians of Bolivia still speak the language of their Inca ancestors and live in solid granite houses built long ago. But they no longer decorate their homes with geometric, golden statues of gods inlaid with precious stones as the Incas did.

Materials: plaster of Paris, small container such as a plastic yoghourt pot, small pointed knife, soup spoon, pin, match, aluminium foil, nail varnish or paint and spirit varnish, brush and white spirit to clean it, very fine glass paper.

Trace and cut out the shapes of the figures above. Mix five level soup spoons of plaster of Paris and two spoons of water in the pot. This quantity will make two pendants or one bas-relief.

Pendants: spread the plaster over a piece of foil with the knife to form a rectangle of 13×8 cm/$5\frac{1}{4} \times 3\frac{1}{4}$″. Hold the drawings over the plaster and prick out the outlines with a pin. Cut them out with a knife and add the details with the matchstick or a pin. Remember to make a hole to hang the pendants. Leave to dry for four to six hours and smooth the edges with glass paper before painting. Paint with two coats of nail varnish, or two coats of paint and one of varnish and leave to dry.

Bas relief: spread half the plaster over the foil and make a figure as above. Mix the remaining plaster and form a plaque larger than the figure. Smooth with the blade of the knife and make a hole if you wish to hang it on the wall. Leave to dry for four hours. Then mix one spoon of plaster and a few drops of water, fill in any crevices on the back of the figure, wet the plaque and put on the figure. Leave to dry flat.

BRAZIL Carnival maracas

Once a year all the people of Rio de Janeiro join together for three days of carnival culminating on Shrove Tuesday when they dance through the streets in fantastic costumes. The music is played on guitars and drums, coloured by the distinctive South American sound of rhythm instruments like these *maracas* which they make out of hollowed gourds.

Materials: for one *maraca*, one and a half cardboard egg boxes, Polycell paste, basin, soup spoon, a small round balloon, 50 cm/20" of thin string, cellulose wadding, about 25 cm/10" bamboo; seeds (here fifteen pop corn seeds) or small pebbles, pliable cardboard measuring 5×2 cm/$2 \times \frac{3}{4}$", Evostik, glass paper, paint, spirit varnish, brush and white spirit for cleaning.

Make the papier mâché according to the instructions for Indian bracelets on page 48. When it is ready, blow up the balloon till it measures about 33 cm/13" round. Tie the balloon tightly with string and leave the ends hanging. Cut some small pieces of cellulose wadding and glue them onto the piece of cardboard to make a pipe 2 cm/$\frac{3}{4}$" long which will fit round the bamboo.

Cover the balloon in papier mâché, starting at the top. When you get near the neck of the balloon, slip the pipe over the string up to the end of the balloon and continue applying the papier mâché over it. Make sure the surface is as smooth as possible, adding extra glue and paper if necessary, then coat the whole thing with glue and hang up to dry for about forty-eight hours.

When the papier mâché is dry, burst the balloon and pull it out. Put the seeds or stones inside. Coat the inside of the pipe and the end of the bamboo with Evostik and insert the bamboo into the pipe. If it wiggles at all, stuff a little glued cellulose wadding inside the pipe to hold it firm. Rub the whole thing with glass paper, paint it, add a design (there is one suggestion on this page) and varnish.

CANADA Paper-weight

As the world's largest exporter of timber it is not surprising that Canada should have chosen the maple leaf as its national symbol. The tree also produces a delicious syrup which was widely used as a sweetener by the Indians and the early settlers.

Materials: freshly gathered maple or plane leaves, plaster of Paris, small plastic pot, soup spoon, teaspoon, flat brush 1 cm/$\frac{5}{8}$" wide, red and yellow paint, varnish and white spirit to clean the brush, small pointed knife, very fine metal file or glass paper, white cord or string if desired.

The maple leaf is the symbol of Canada, but you can use any leaves as long as they are fresh and whole.

Cover your working area with paper and lay two or three leaves on it, ribs uppermost. Mix five level teaspoons of plaster of Paris with two teaspoons of water in the pot and cover the leaves with this mixture with the flat brush. Do not try to press the leaves flat and be careful not to spread the plaster over the edges.

As soon as this layer is dry, mix five level soup spoons of plaster of Paris with two soup spoons of water and leave to settle for a little while. Wet the dry plaster and pour another layer over the leaves, smoothing it out with the brush till this second layer is about 5 mm/$\frac{1}{4}$" deep. If you go over the edge, remove the excess with the point of the knife. Add a little more plaster to the centre back to strengthen it and if you want to hang the leaf up put in a loop of cord (see diagram). Leave to dry for two hours before carefully removing the leaf; then leave for another three to four hours. File or rub away any bumps on the back. When painting, work with plenty of water. Coat with two layers of varnish.

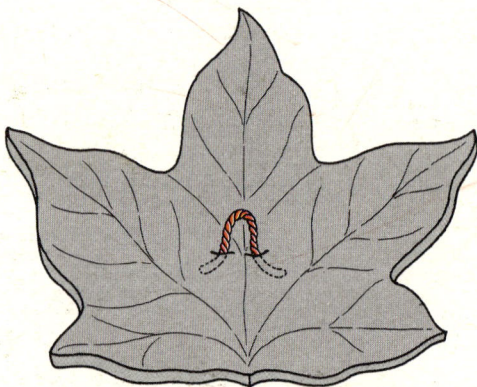

64

COLOMBIA

Golden mask

The goldsmiths of Colombia were renowned for their skill and, although most of their treasures were melted down by the Spanish conquerors in the sixteenth and seventeenth centuries, many people still believe in the existence of El Dorado, a hidden store of gold and precious stones. Masks like this one were often attached to mummies before burial.

Materials: a piece of fine sheet metal or aluminium foil measuring 30 × 25 cm/12 × 10", Araldite glue, scissors, hammer, large nail, small pointed knife, wax crayon, tracing paper, sticky tape.

Trace the mask from the diagram and transfer the design to the sheet metal with a wax crayon. Make sure you do all the work on the back of the mask because the metal marks easily.

Cut out the eyes and mouth by making a hole with the point of the knife and putting the scissors through it. Still working on the back, mark the decorative lines and the mouth with the point of the knife and the flowers by tapping the head of the nail with the hammer.

Trace and cut out two top and two bottom sets of eyelashes and the nose. Fringe the eyelashes and fold the nose along the dotted lines (see diagram). The projection A on the nose should pass through the hole A on the mask and the projection B. The nostrils are curved round and held in place by the base.

Make sure the pieces fit properly before making up the glue. Stick on the base of the eyelashes and those of the nose to the back of the mask, hold in place with sticky tape and leave to dry for at least four hours. Remove any traces of wet glue with a damp rag. When the glue is completely dry, take off the sticky tape, scrape off any remaining glue with a knife, bend back the eyelashes and bend the ears slightly forwards. This mask can be worn or mounted on painted card or card covered with dark fabric.

top lashes

bottom lashes

A

B

A

B'

half nose

UNITED STATES Patchwork cushion

The oldest piece of patchwork in existence is an Egyptian funeral pall over 3000 years old, but more famous, perhaps, is the work of the English and Dutch pioneering women of America who produced a great variety of patterns using different templates (pieces of metal or card cut into the desired geometrical shape).

Materials: pieces of material of similar texture, stiff paper, pencil, sewing thread, needles, scissors, kapok or foam chips.

Chequered cushion: you can make this with a piece of plain fabric measuring 50 × 50 cm/20 × 20″ and an old tie. Undo the tie and press it flat. Then cut five squares measuring about 10 × 10 cm/4 × 4″, depending on the size of the tie. Cut the same number (and size) of squares in plain fabric and sew the two kinds of pieces together alternately, right sides together. Place the finished patchwork on a piece of plain fabric cut to the same size.

Pin the two pieces together, right sides facing inwards. Sew round three and a half sides. Turn the material right side out, stuff with kapok and finish sewing together.

Flowered cushion: this is made of hexagons (see fig. 1 for basic shape). Use fabric of matching colours and the same texture. You can make the cushion in different sizes by copying either the photograph or fig. 2. Draw the hexagons onto the back of the fabric, allow 1 cm/⅜″ extra for hem and cut out. Join the pieces with right sides together. Fill the gaps round the edges with triangles (coloured blue-grey in fig. 2). Place the patchwork on a piece of plain fabric and cut to the same size. Join back and front, right sides together, leaving side AB open. Turn right side out, stuff with kapok or foam and sew up the opening.

Star cushion: this is not true patchwork, but appliqué. You will need two squares of fabric with sides of 44 cm/18″, a piece 10 × 10 cm/4 × 4″ in the same fabric and six different pieces of patterned material at least 12 × 12 cm/5 × 5″. Copy the shape in fig. 3 onto stiff paper, pin onto one of the pieces of patterned material, baste round the outline allowing 1 cm/⅜″ all round for hem and cut out. Do the same with the other five pieces. Join the six pieces to form a star and place them on a circular centre piece 8 cm/3¼″ in diameter cut from the small plain piece of material. Turn under the points of the star, pin carefully to the centre of one of the large pieces of fabric and sew on. Then make up the cushion as already described.

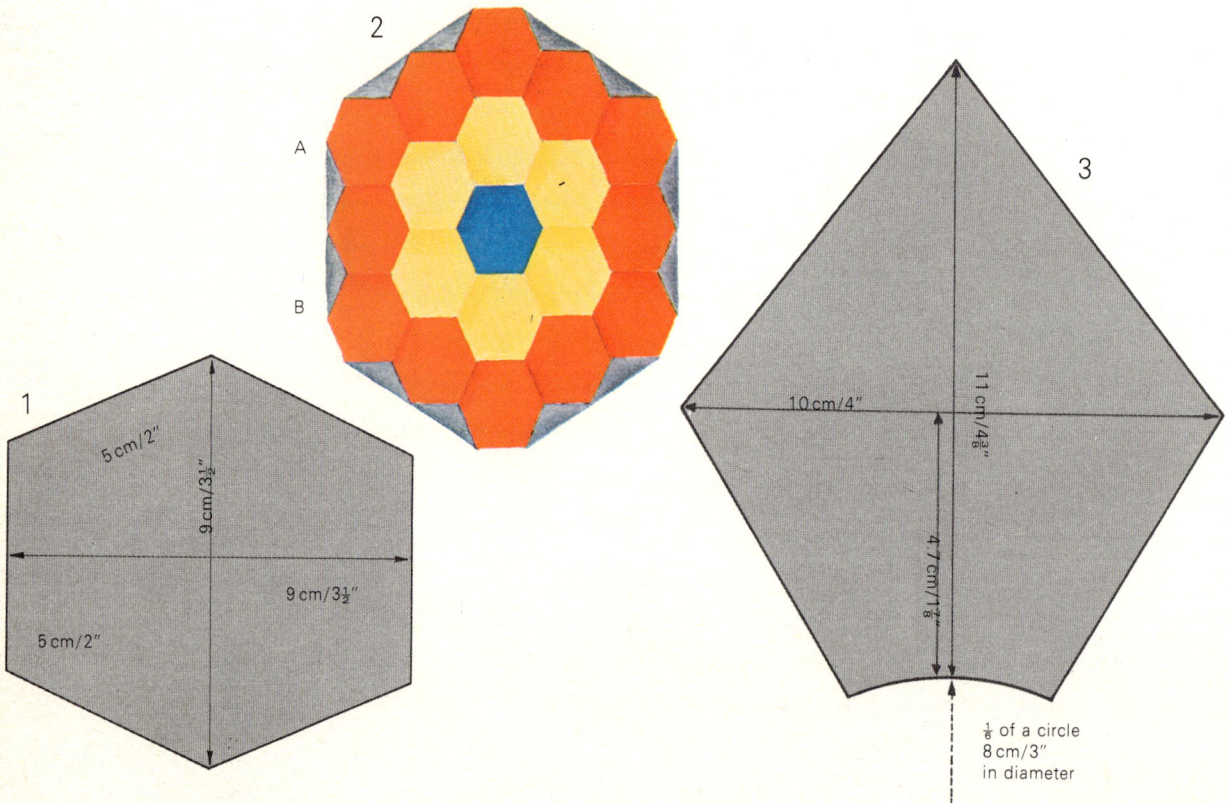

2

A

B

1

5 cm/2″

9 cm/3½″

9 cm/3½″

5 cm/2″

5 cm/2″

3

10 cm/4″

11 cm/4⅜″

4.7 cm/1⅞″

⅛ of a circle 8 cm/3″ in diameter

MEXICO Sun god

The design for this wall hanging was inspired by the work of the Huichol Indians of western Mexico who make beautiful woollen textiles. Their ancestors used to worship the sun and even made human sacrifices to it. Although the present-day Mexicans are Christian, they still make woollen god's eyes to ward off devils.

Materials: piece of strong cardboard or hardboard measuring 40 × 40 cm/16 × 16", thick wool in various colours, including at least $\frac{1}{3}$ of a ball for the background (here royal blue), a heavy object to use as a press, knitting needle or other pointed object, compasses, ruler, pencil, vinyl glue, small, fine-toothed saw if needed.

Following the measurements on the diagram below, draw the pattern on the background. The sun has twenty-four rays, each divided in two.

Start with the eyes and mouth. Blob some glue on the area you will be filling, then coil the wool round carefully without pulling too hard. Place under the press before going on to the next stage and keep the press moving round after you as you work. Fill the gaps in the inner-most circle, then lay the wool round the sun's face in rings to fill the circle marked B. On the last row of B take the background wool out along the line C, round the point of the knitting needle and back to B to form the rays.

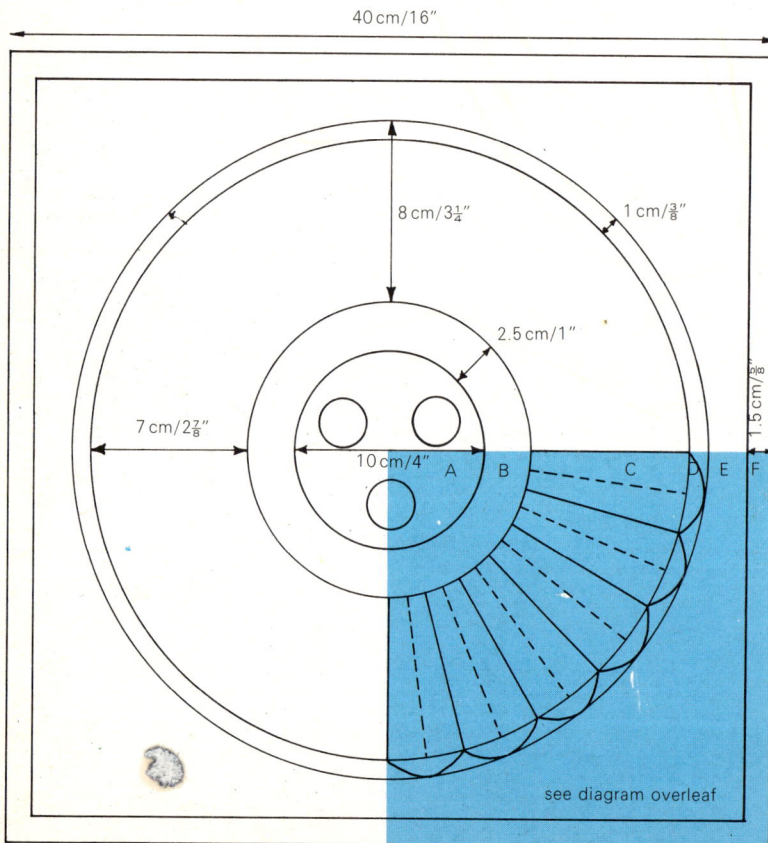

40 cm/16"

8 cm/$3\frac{1}{4}$"

1 cm/$\frac{3}{8}$"

2.5 cm/1"

7 cm/$2\frac{7}{8}$"

1.5 cm/$\frac{5}{8}$"

10 cm/4" A B C D E F

see diagram overleaf

Toucan: make this design in toning shades of different colours on thick white card. Draw the bird on the card and start filling the wing (here yellow) by coiling the wool round carefully. Then go backwards and forwards until you have finished the oval shape and fill the areas left by the main outlines.

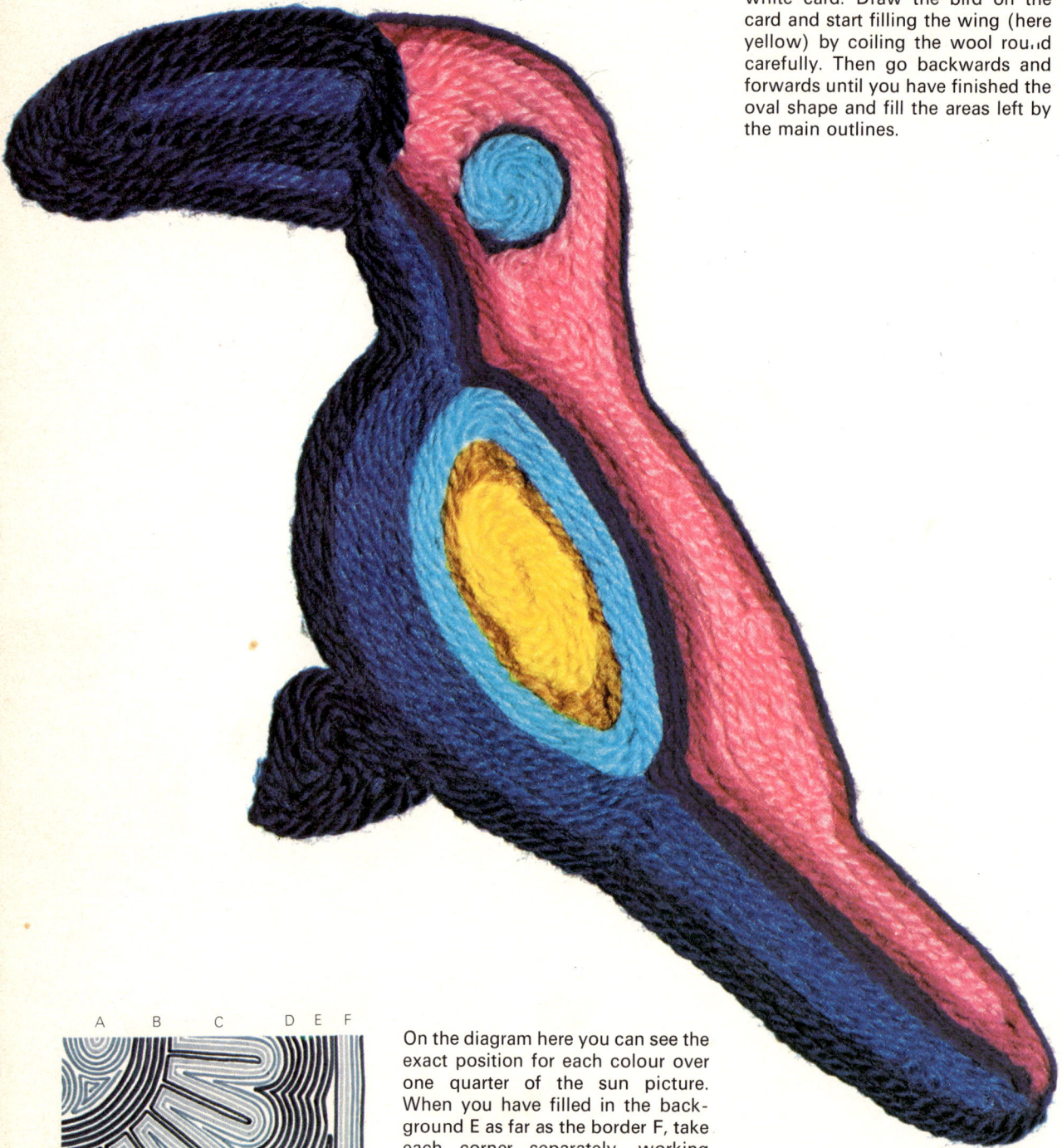

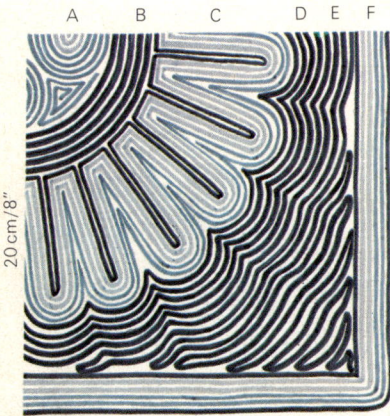

A   B   C   D E F

20 cm/8"

On the diagram here you can see the exact position for each colour over one quarter of the sun picture. When you have filled in the background E as far as the border F, take each corner separately, working backwards and forwards out to the point of the corner. Then make the border and round off the corners with a saw, if you wish. To hang up the picture, glue a piece of linen cord to the back.

PERU Purse

The Indians of the Andes carry bags slung across their backs on their journeys over the mountains, much as their Inca ancestors did. Nowadays Peruvian craftsmen use a similar design to make small purses. The motif on this one represents a South American plant which grows in the form of a candlestick to heights of over sixty feet.

Materials: pieces of fabric in two different colours (here two pieces measuring 20 × 12 cm/8 × 5" in turquoise and one piece 12 × 8 cm/5 × 3" in pink), gold thread, two threads of thick wool, 45 cm/18" long, threads to match the wool and the gold thread, paper, scissors, pencil, pins.

Draw the basic shape in fig. 1 on the paper. Fold one of the larger pieces of fabric in two to measure 12 × 10 cm/5 × 4" and pin on the pattern, placing the line AB along the fold. Add 3 mm/⅛" seam allowance all round and cut out. Repeat on the other large piece of fabric. You will then have the two pieces numbered 1 and 2 in fig. 2. Oversew the raw edges and sew running stitches along the fold AB. Cut out the pink piece shown in figs. 2–3 and draw on the design. Appliqué the gold thread with gold coloured cotton, following the direction of the arrows in fig. 1. Sew on the gold border looping the thread as shown in fig. 3. Turn down the top edge of the small (pink) piece of fabric and stitch it onto one of the larger (blue) pieces along the line CD. Place the two larger pieces together (figs. 2, 4) and stitch round through all thicknesses to form a bag. Oversew with gold thread. Thread two strings round the top, one above the other starting from opposite sides, as shown in fig. 1. Tie all four ends together and bind the knot with gold thread.

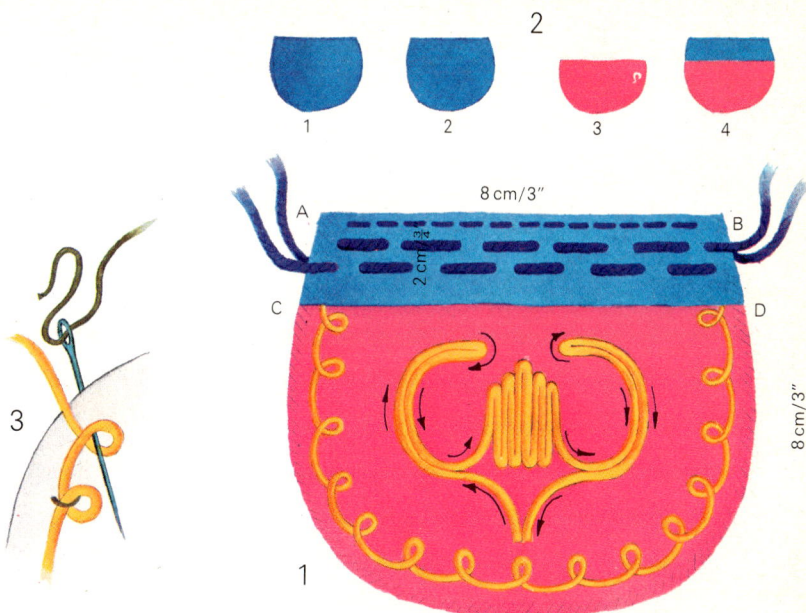

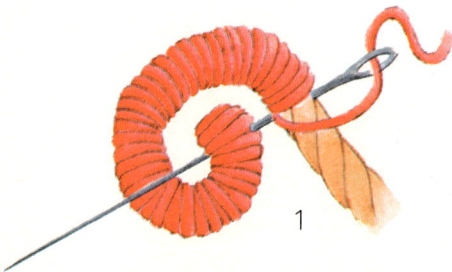

1

2

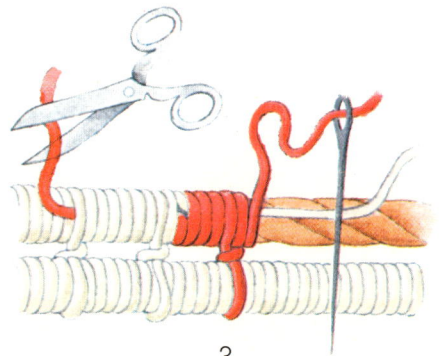

3

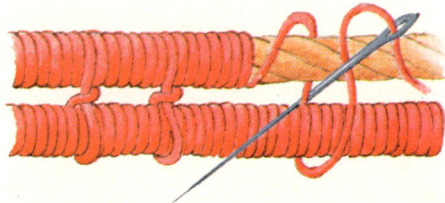

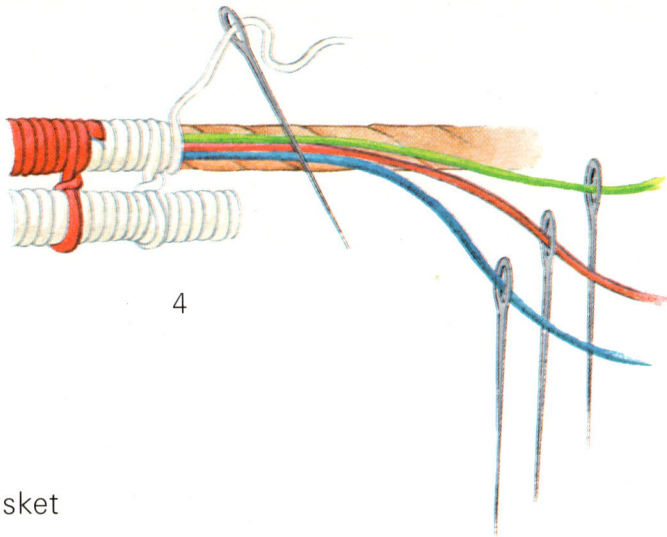

4

Africa

ALGERIA String basket

The technique of paper-making was brought from the Far East by the Arabs with the Chinese prisoners they took at Samarkand in the eighth century. One of the best quality papers in use today is made from esparto grass which grows in Algeria. The local people, however, also use it to make cord and rope, which craftsmen sew into baskets.

Materials: 12 m/13$\frac{1}{2}$ yards of 3 mm/ $\frac{1}{8}$" thick string, a ball of thin white string about 100 m/110 yards long, three balls of fine, coloured string (here red, green and blue) for the pattern, as many large-eyed needles as you have coloured strings, scissors.

Begin in the middle of the basket by winding some thin string (here red) round the thick string and shaping it into a coil. Once you have formed one whole circle proceed as follows: wind the thin string round the thick four to six times, pass the needle under the preceding row (fig. 1), then between the two rows (fig. 2) and start again. Fig. 3 shows what to do with the ends of string when you wish to change colours.

To make the pattern illustrated work seven rounds in red, one in green and one in white. Divide the white round into six equal parts and on the next round wind the blue string round four times at each of the six points, catching it under the white string when not in use. Similarly, when you start adding the other colours, keep them next to the thick string as in fig. 4. Continue with the star pattern shown in fig. 5 until you reach the end of the last green point, then work two rounds in white, taper the thick string and fasten off.

To make the sides of the basket, hold the base towards you and continue the pattern up to the desired height.

With different thicknesses of string you can make all kinds of things using this technique; very large mats, for example, coasters or jewel boxes.

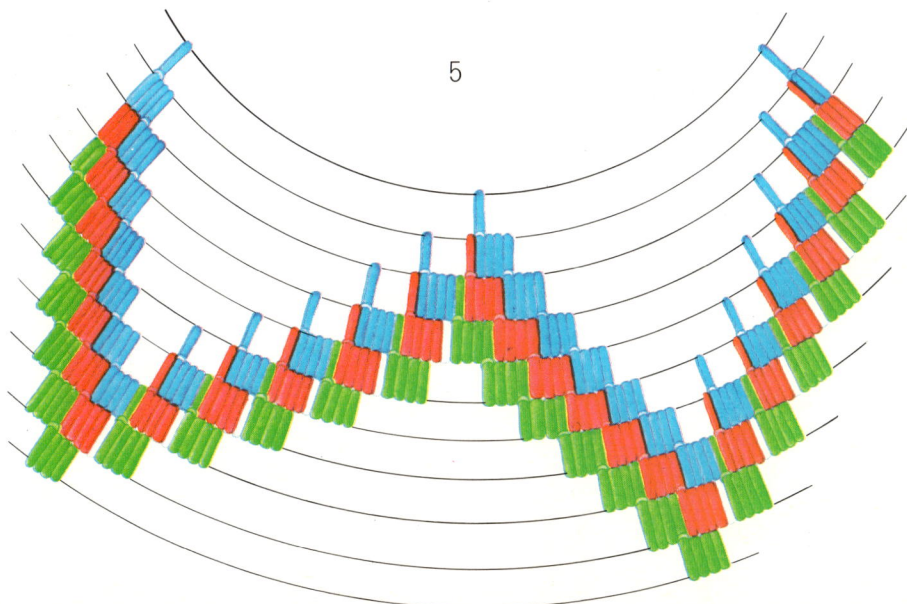

5

MOROCCO Braided belt

0

1

2

3

plaiting eight threads

The Berber women who make belts like these to sell in the souks, or covered markets, of North Africa, enjoy much greater freedom than other Muslim women. For the Berbers, the original inhabitants of the area north of the Sahara, have kept their own traditions, even their own alphabet, although many of them have abandoned their no-madic life to earn a living from agriculture and village handicrafts.

Materials: eight lengths of wool 4 m/4½ yards long for each plait (here four plaits of different colours: violet, yellow, orange and green, made of tapestry wool), scissors, fine silk thread in various colours, needle, tape measure.

If your wool is very thick you can make a belt from only two or three plaits. The basic method for plait-ing eight threads together is shown on this page with a different colour for each thread to make it easy to follow. Tie the threads together and hook the knot onto something firm like a window catch. Start with fig. 0, holding four threads out to each side. Note that these four always return to their original side of the work after plaiting. Fig. 1: take the violet thread from the far right across the other three threads on the right, under the two threads left of centre and leave in the centre right. Pull tight. Fig. 2: take the brown thread from the far left across the other three left hand threads, under the two threads right of centre and leave at the centre left. Repeat from fig. 1 taking the far right thread, then the far left as in fig. 2 and so on. Keep the threads wound in balls so that they do not get tangled.

Finish the plait with a knot. When you have made the required number of plaits fold the whole lot in two. Make a slip knot, leaving a loop of about 6 cm/6½" at the folded end and bind the knot and the loop with silk thread. Make another knot 5 cm/2" from the first one. Lay the plaits out flat and measure along 25 cm/10" from the second knot. Bind the plaits together at this point with silk as shown in fig. 4. Use different coloured silk threads and bind for 3 cm/1¼", alternating the colours. Repeat 40 cm/16" further on. Measure another 30 cm/12", make another knot covered in silk and divide the belt into two or three parts, each finished in a knot covered in silk with tassels 6 cm/2½" long.

To wear the belt, pass it round your waist, thread the tasselled end through the loop and leave the ends hanging.

4

silk binding

TUNISIA Lucky fish

The fish was a sacred symbol in Middle Eastern countries long before the Christians adopted it as a secret sign of recognition. Indeed, some of the ancient myths of the creation made the fish the first living creature. In Tunisia the people still hang brightly coloured fish on their walls to ward off bad luck.

Materials: tracing paper, pencil, pins, vinyl glue, thin cardboard, pieces of velvet and sewing thread to match them, canvas, strong white thread, about 1 m/1 yard white braid, depending on the size of the fish, sequins, small beads, coloured foil (from sweets or chocolates), scraps of canvas, needles, cotton wool.

Trace the large fish on this page, pin onto the material and cut out one in velvet and one in canvas. Glue both pieces separately to thin cardboard and cut out. Cut the diamond shape for the head from velvet of a different colour, pink the edges which will lie over the inside of the fish to avoid fraying and stitch it in place. Mark the head and tail shapes in white braid, stitching along the centre of the braid. Decorate the velvet fish with sequins held in place by a small bead and make up a design with foil to be glued on. Place the velvet and canvas fishes card sides together and pin. Sew the braid carefully to the top of the head through all thicknesses, leave a length to hang the fish up by and start sewing again at the top of the tail. When you reach the mouth loop the braid and stuff the fish with cotton wool, pushing it well in with a pencil before continuing with the braid.

When making the small fishes, decorate the velvet fish, then stick it to one side of a piece of cardboard and the canvas fish to the other.

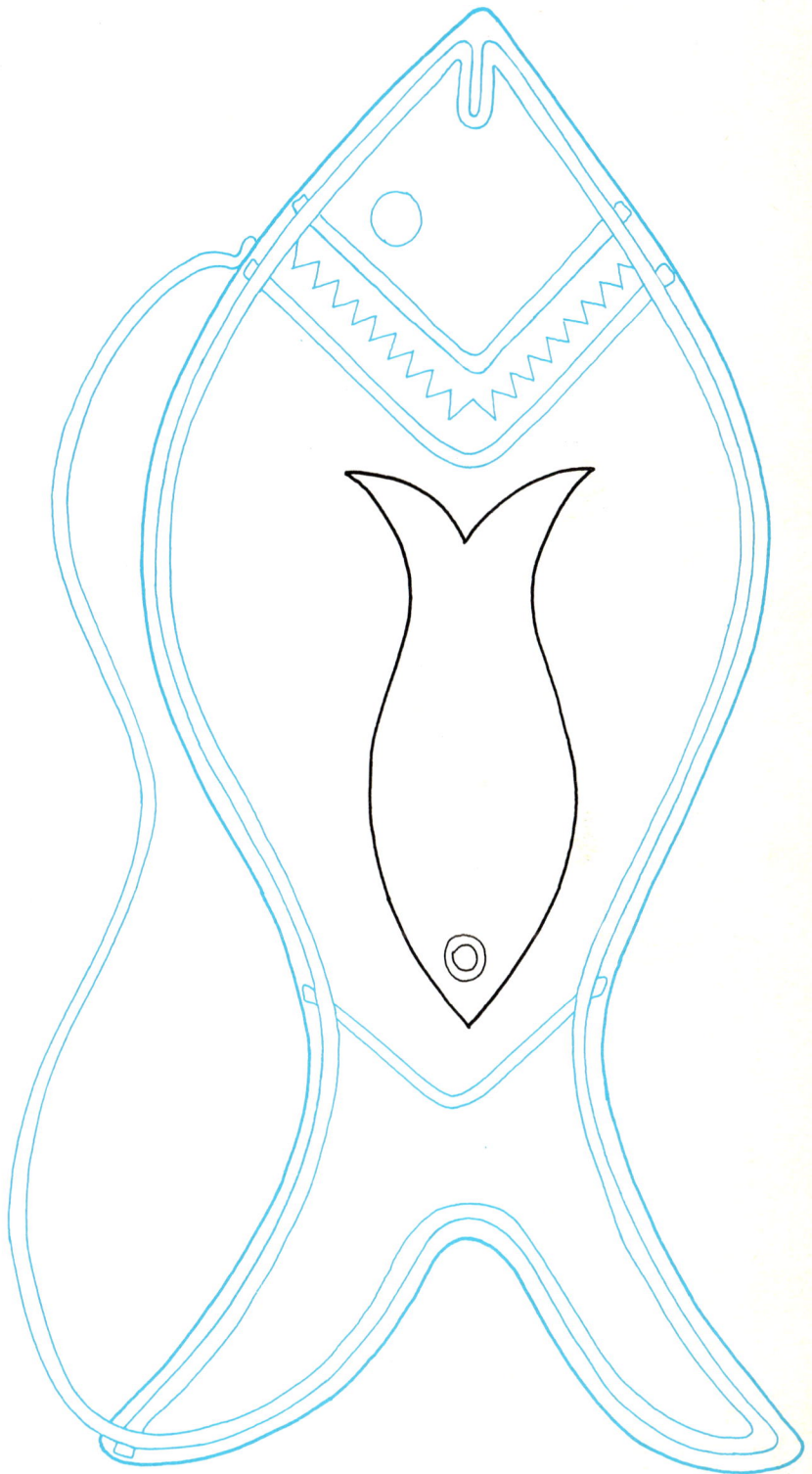

CAMEROONS Bead bonanza

Small glass beads first came to Africa with European explorers and traders. By the height of the terrible traffic in slaves across the Atlantic traders were paying a mere four pounds of beads for one human life. In the Cameroons, the women decorate all kinds of things with beads, especially bottles, calabashes, drums and baskets.

Materials: small curved bottle (see photograph), about 30 × 25 cm/ 12 × 10" of hessian or other coarse woven fabric, about 120 g/5 oz rocaille beads 2–3 mm/about $\frac{1}{8}$" in diameter (30 g/1$\frac{1}{4}$ oz in each of four colours), light linen thread, needles, thimble, pliers, cork 3.5 cm/1$\frac{1}{2}$" long, tailor's chalk, compasses, scissors, vinyl glue, small knife, pencil.

Adapt the pattern below to suit the height and diameter of your bottle and cut out the fabric. Coat with a thin layer of glue and stick the fabric to the bottle. Notch the bottom of the fabric and fold it over the base, then cover with a circular piece of fabric.

Divide the bottle into six equal parts and mark with pencil. Thread the needle, knot the end of the thread and make a stitch in the fabric as close as possible to the neck of the bottle. Thread on as many beads as you need to reach the next pencil mark, make a stitch in the fabric and knot the thread round as shown in fig. 2. Continue with beads of a different colour. Make a chequered pattern in three colours, working four rows for the first square, six for the next, and so on up to twelve. (See the photograph opposite.) Use the pliers to help pull the needle through if it gets too stiff.

Then thread on a stripe 1.5 cm/$\frac{3}{4}$" deep of beads the same colour (here red). Continue in red, adding one blue bead at each pencil mark and work down the blue, yellow and black pattern.

Shape the bottom 1.5 cm/$\frac{3}{4}$" of the cork to fit in the bottle. Glue two pieces of fabric measuring 6 × 2 cm/2$\frac{1}{2}$ × 1$\frac{1}{4}$" in an X across the top. Take another piece measuring 14 × 4 cm/5$\frac{1}{2}$" × 1$\frac{3}{4}$", fold in two lengthwise, cover in glue and wrap round the cork with the fold at the top. Sew on the beads in a coil starting from the centre top and working down the sides, anchoring the two-coloured handle as you go.

1

2

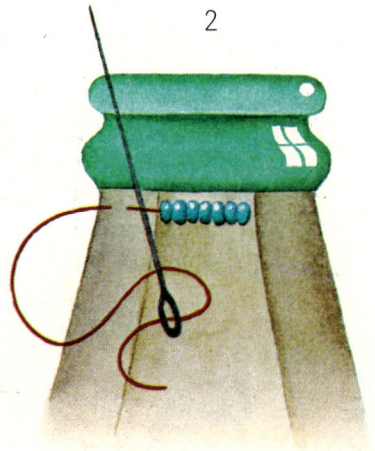

DAHOMEY Wall hanging

In Dahomey houses the walls are hung with huge tapestries which tell the history of local chiefs in symbols. The pineapple, for example, was the symbol of King Aglongo who reigned at the end of the eighteenth century. He was supposed to have taken shelter from a storm under a palm tree. The tree was blown down but the king was unharmed, just as a small pineapple growing beside a palm tree might be.

Materials: piece of material, black or white, measuring 75 × 45 cm/ 30 × 18", pieces of plain coloured fabric with thread to match, tracing paper, two small curtain rings, large piece of squared paper.

Enlarge the designs illustrated opposite by dividing the squared paper into squares of 4 cm/1⅝" and carefully copying the outlines of the motifs in the corresponding squares. Trace each of the smaller pieces that go to make up the designs and pin the tracings onto the different coloured fabrics.

Cut out the pieces as you need them to avoid unnecessary fraying. Sew the features onto the buffalo before stitching the whole animal to the background. Use an overcasting stitch and a coloured thread to match the piece you are sewing on. If the piece is fairly large, tack it in position first.

Quilt the pineapple by machining or sewing squares across it and make large stitches in white thread for the buffalo's teeth. Turn up 2.5 cm/ 1" all round the background and hem. Attach the curtain rings, one at each top corner, for hanging the picture up.

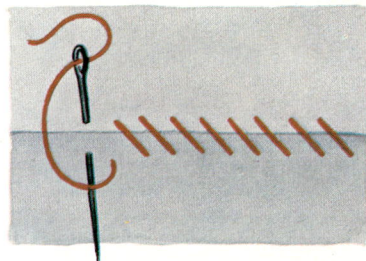

KENYA Warrior's necklace

The Masai people live along the Great Rift Valley of Kenya and Tanzania. They live entirely on the cattle they breed and have a strong warrior tradition. The young men still have to undergo a period of military service within the tribe during which time they live apart from their families. Not until this is accomplished can they marry or take part in the government of the tribe.

Materials: about 70 g/3 oz rocaille beads of 2 mm/$\frac{1}{16}$" (here 30 g/1$\frac{1}{4}$ oz orange, 30 g/1$\frac{1}{4}$ oz green, 5 g/$\frac{1}{4}$ oz white and 5 g/$\frac{1}{4}$ oz navy blue), a bobbin of brass wire, a lace of natural coloured leather, piece of fine leather the same colour measuring 6 × 3 cm/2$\frac{1}{2}$ × 1$\frac{3}{8}$", leather needle or large needle fixed in a cork, scissors, pliers, Evostik, eight clothes pegs, thimble, newspaper, a round oblong bead measuring about 5 to 7 mm/$\frac{3}{16}$ to $\frac{1}{4}$" for the ring.

Necklace: cut seven pieces of leather lacing each 5 cm/2" long and make eighteen equidistant holes along the widest edge with the needle wedged in the thimble.

Cut four thongs of fine leather measuring 5 × 0.6 cm/2 × $\frac{1}{4}$" and make eighteen equidistant holes in two of them. Cut 40 cm/16" wire for the first row and progressively more for each successive row. Thread the wire through the top hole of one of the thongs and twist back the end on the wrong side with the pliers as shown in fig. 1. Thread on twenty-seven beads (here green), then thread on the top hole of the first piece of leather lacing, then twenty-seven more beads, then the second piece of lacing and so on to the last thong of fine leather. Wind the wire twice round tightly and cut. Repeat for each of the eighteen holes following the order of colours in fig. 1 (or any order you please), increasing the number of beads so that the necklace lies flat.

Make a fastener as shown in fig. 2 and attach it to the ends of wire on the thongs. Take the two remaining, unholed pieces of fine leather, make two holes in either end of them so that you can decorate them with two rows of beads as in fig. 3 and glue them wrong sides together

onto the other thongs. Take care to cover all ends of wire. Hold with clothes pegs until dry.

Ring: make a hook on the end of a piece of brass wire 50 cm/20" long. Thread on the large bead and however many small beads you need to go round your finger. Thread the wire back through the large bead as in fig. 4A, wind the hooked end round it and cut. Pull the wire tight and thread on a half circle of beads. Wind the wire tightly round the ring between the large bead and the first of the small beads, then thread on the other half circle (fig. 4B). Continue in this way until there are four circles, each attached a little further down the base. Finish by winding the wire tightly round the base twice and cutting.

1

2

3

4

MALAGASY Coil belt

Malagasy, or Madagascar as it was called until recently, is an island rich in tropical vegetation. One of the plants which grows there has large fleshy leaves which are processed into stiff, bristly fibres for making the twine we call sisal. These can be woven into particularly hard-wearing carpets.

Materials: a ball of sisal twine, beige linen thread, needle, scissors. For dyeing: cold dye, fixative and basin.

For one coil cut 80 cm/32" of twine. Thread the needle and push it through one end of the string. Make three or four half hitches as shown in fig. 1. Then coil the twine on a flat surface keeping the rounds tight. Hold the sisal together by stitching through at least two thicknesses of twine at one time. Make a couple more half hitches at the end to stop fraying then fasten off. A belt takes about twelve coils.

Take the rest of the ball of twine and, leaving a loose end of 25 cm/ 10", stitch the coils along it side by side. Measure another 25 cm/10" and cut.

Finish the ends with tassels. To make one tassel, cut four lengths of twine each 15 cm/6" long. Tie them to the end of the belt with linen thread (fig. 2A), fold over and bind the top of the tassel with more thread (fig. 2B). Unravel the twine and trim the ends.

To colour, leave the belt in a dye bath for fifteen minutes, rinse well and dry flat on absorbent paper.

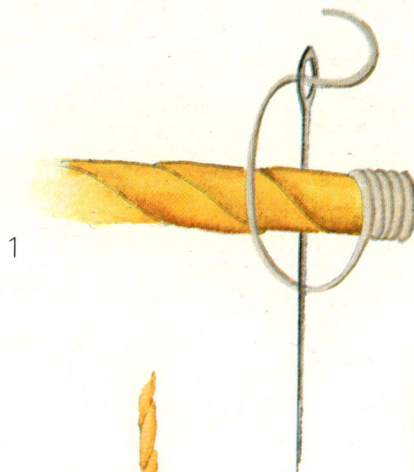

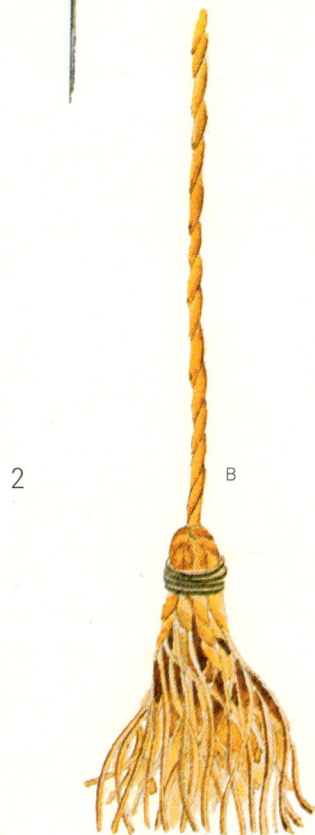

Oceania

MELANESIA Hat mask

This mask is an exact copy of one found in New Britain, an island off the coast of New Guinea. It was worn as a badge of recognition by the members of a secret society. Masks were also used to represent mythological characters and departed relatives, and even, among some tribes, to distinguish the local police force.

Materials: piece of cardboard 40 × 40 cm/16 × 16″, chicken feathers (ask a poulterer), ruler, string 40 cm/16″ long, pencil, strong thread, awl or large needle fixed in a cork, natural coloured raffia, black insulating tape or sticky tape, glue, black and white poster paint, brush, two clothes pegs.

Using the string and following the instructions on fig. 1, draw an arc with a 40 cm/16″ radius on the cardboard. Cut off a triangle 4 cm/1½″ from the centre corner of the cardboard and draw another triangle (BCD), making the line CD measure 7 cm/3″. The measurement from E to D should fit round your head, so adjust this if necessary before cutting out. 1.5 cm/⅝″ from the line AB make two holes 1.5 cm/⅝″ apart. Punch holes all along the line ED 1 cm/⅜″ from the edge and the same distance apart and thread a piece of raffia in each hole by folding it in two, passing the loop through the hole and drawing the ends through the loop (fig. 2). Tie the feathers into a firm bunch with the string and attach by threading the string a few times through the holes at A and B.

Coat the triangle BCD with glue and stick to the other side to form a cone with D lying directly under E. Tape along the join and secure with clothes pegs until the glue is dry. Then draw the nose, eyebrows, eyes and mouth on the front of the cone, as shown below, and paint in carefully with two coats of black and white. When you put on the hat, the raffia will hide your face and most of your body.

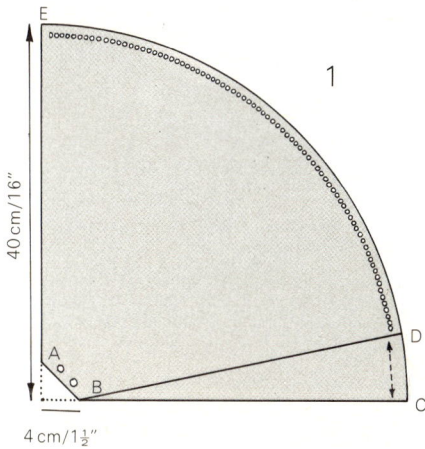

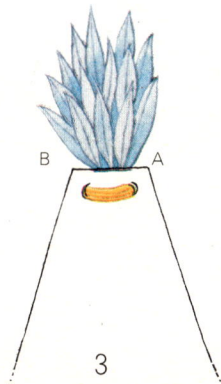

POLYNESIA Lei

The islands of the South Seas seemed like paradise to the first European sailors who reached there. Fruit and flowers grew in natural abundance, the sand was white and fringed with palm trees and the islanders welcomed them with songs and garlands called *leis*.

Materials: two wrapped packets of crêpe paper, one white and one red, scissors, ruler, table knife, needle, strong thread, pipe cleaner or small stick 7 cm/3" long for the flower worn in the ear.

Lei: take the label off the crêpe paper, but do not unfold the paper. It should be just over 10 cm/4" wide. Cut across all thicknesses of the paper about 7 cm/3" from the bottom. Make four cuts 5 cm/2" deep into this strip, at the intervals shown by the solid lines in fig. 1A. Unfold the paper. Twist all the narrowest fringes, 1 cm/⅜" wide, up to a point between your finger and thumb. Gently smooth out the other strips with the blade of the knife till they curl up (fig. 2). Cut the length of fringe in half and each half will make one flower. For a

child's *lei* you will need three red and three white flowers, for an adult four red and four white. Cut a piece of thread about 2 m/7' long and thread it double into a large needle. Gather along the bottom of the fringing as shown in fig. 2, threading on red and white strips alternately. Tie the end of the thread to something firm and pull up each strip to form a flower. Arrange the flowers along the thread and tie the ends together at the required length.

Single flower: cut a rectangle of crêpe paper measuring 30 × 15 cm/ 12 × 6" and fold in four as shown in fig. 3. Cut out the petal shape, unfold the paper and smooth the petals towards you with the blade of the knife. Cut another rectangle 20 × 6 cm/8 × 2¼" and clip three strips 10 cm/4" long and 2 cm/¾" wide (fig. 4). Twist the strips to form stamens and gather the four petals round the bottom of the stamens at the line AB on fig. 4, leaving the part shaded on the diagram hanging free. Make one stitch into the bottom of the flower and wind the thread round it a few

times. Take a pipe cleaner or stick and push it into the extra piece. Cut a strip of paper measuring 15 × 2 cm/6 × 1" and wind it round the stem.

According to tradition, you should wear the flower over your left ear if you have already lost your heart to someone, over the right ear if you have not.

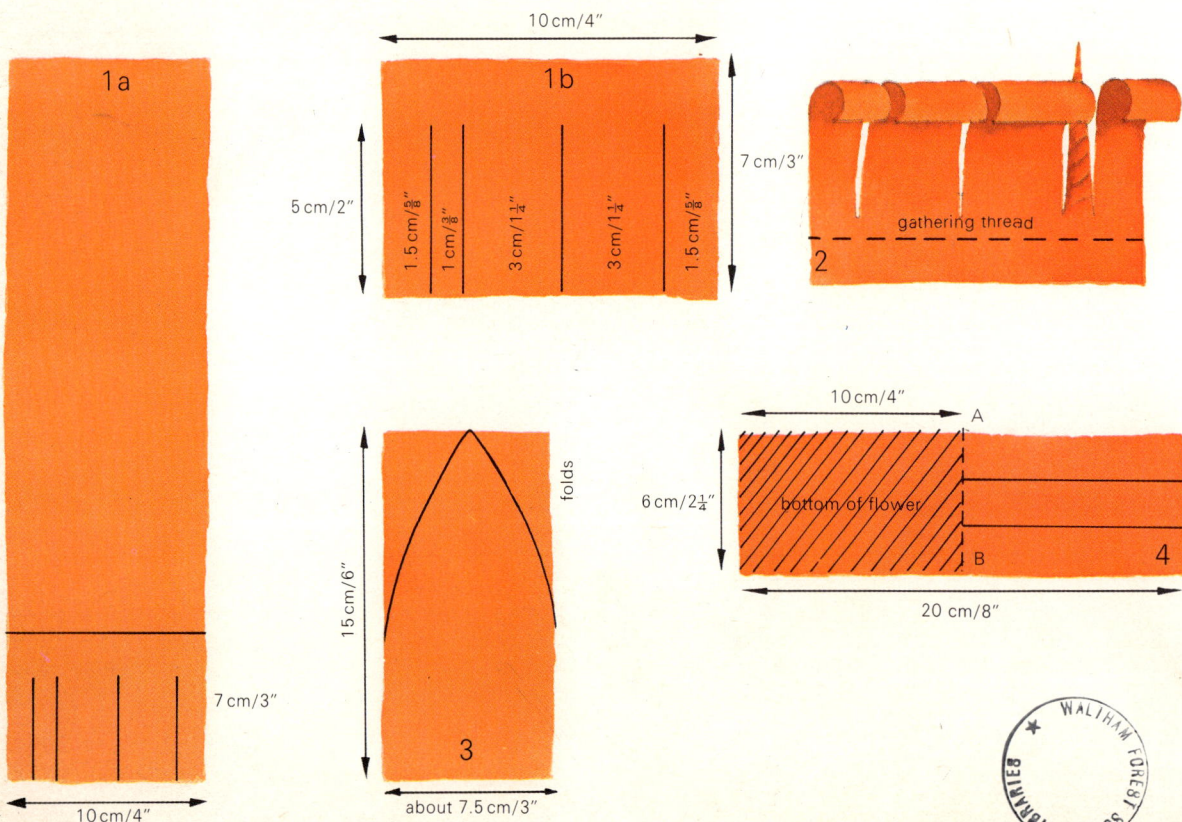

1a

10 cm/4"

1b

5 cm/2"

1.5 cm/⅝" 1 cm/⅜" 3 cm/1¼" 3 cm/1¼" 1.5 cm/⅝"

7 cm/3"

gathering thread

2

7 cm/3"

10 cm/4"

15 cm/6"

folds

3

about 7.5 cm/3"

10 cm/4"

A

6 cm/2¼"   bottom of flower

B

4

20 cm/8"